FROM
SENTENCE
TO PARAGRAPH

FROM SENTENCE TO PARAGRAPH

A WRITING WORKBOOK IN
ENGLISH AS A SECOND LANGUAGE

Robert G. Bander

HOLT, RINEHART AND WINSTON
New York   Chicago   San Francisco
Atlanta   Dallas   Montreal   Toronto

Library of Congress Cataloging in Publication Data

Bander, Robert G.
  From sentence to paragraph.

  Includes index.
  1. English language — Text-books for foreigners.
2. English language — Rhetoric.   I. Title.
PE1128.B298 808′.042 79-2558

ISBN 0-03-045641-X

Excerpts used on pp. 12, 16 (Act. 3), 18 (Acts. 4 & 5), 87, 102 (#3), 103 (#4), 104 (#6), 105 (#7), 106 (#8), 139, 174 (#2), and 193: Used by permission of Nancy Arapoff.

Excerpts used on pp. 94 (#4), 96 (#6 & #7), 98 (#9), 107 (#9), 109 (#10), 152 (Act. 36), 155 (#5), 156 (6), 158 (#8): Doris Wilcox Gilbert, *Breaking the Reading Barrier*,© 1959, pp. 15, 47, 49, 61, 98, 99, 176. Adapted by permission of Prentice-Hall, Inc., Englewood Cliffs, New Jersey.

PREFACE

From Sentence to Paragraph explains English paragraph building in simple terms to lift students to the competency level and beyond in writing. It is a compact book that gives the opportunity for giant-step progress to students who may have come to think of themselves as nonwriters.

Teachers of writing know that perhaps the biggest hurdle of all is bringing their students to the stage of mastering the English paragraph. Vocabulary words can be studied and learned. Grammatical rules can be memorized. Sentences — simple at first, more complex in time — can be formed with practice.

But paragraph control is a subtle concept in any language. In English, it is rooted in unique Anglo-American cultural thought processes; it is developed and refined through extensive exposure to reading. For these reasons, students from cultures other than English-speaking cultures will find the nature of the English paragraph alien. *From Sentence to Paragraph* provides ESL students with a criterion-referenced approach to expressing themselves effectively in English paragraphs.

Many native English-speaking students also find paragraph writing difficult. Those native students whose reading experience has been slight have difficulty understanding when paragraphs begin and end and how they are developed. This text will allow such students to develop their untapped writing skills.

The book is divided into two parts. The first part — *Focus on Sentences* — first introduces students to transitions, those helpers toward smoothly flowing sentences and paragraphs. Then, study of subordination and parallelism draws students beyond their habitual dependence on simple and compound sentence forms. Part 2 — *Focus on Paragraphs* — deals with the four basic principles of paragraph development: the topic sentence, the controlling idea, unity, and coherence. *Four Pre-Writing Steps*, a short introductory section to Part 2, trains students in the key preliminary skills of choosing a topic, narrowing a topic, outlining a paragraph, and forming a topic sentence.

Major features of the book are the three evaluation instruments it contains. First, each chapter provides students with a *Test Yourself* exercise for self-evaluation. Answers to this activity are printed several pages after the exercise. By using this self-test halfway through a chapter, students can realistically pinpoint what they have learned and what they have failed to learn. Doing this allows them to review material early in the chapter before going on to the end-of-the-chapter activities.

Second, each chapter concludes with four to fourteen activities. Answers to these are printed at the end of the book. Since the pages are perforated, instructors who prefer students not to have access to the answers to activities can remove the *Answers to the Activities* pages at the end of the text before books are given out. Perforated pages also allow an instructor to collect assignment pages one at a time, while students retain their books for study and completion of further activities.

Pre- and post-tests are a third evaluation device. To measure overall progress, a Paragraph Writing Pre-Test comes at the beginning of Part 2 and a Paragraph Writing Post-Test comes at the end of Part 2. In addition, a pre-test before and a post-test after each chapter allow both instructor and students to chart learning in small steps from the start to the close of a course.

A four-part appendix contains a glossary of terms used in this book, a list of additional composition topics, forms for writing business letters, and a section of phrasal verbs.

Materials for all of the activities in *From Sentence to Paragraph* cover many areas of interest to students — physics, forestry, languages, rock music, history, mountaineering, economics, automobiles, chemistry, colleges and universities, contact lenses, airplanes, peer relationships. And the lively cartoons that open each chapter express in visual terms the writing concept that the chapter will focus on.

For their assistance in developing this text, I would like to thank Jack Calderon, East Los Angeles College; John F. Clark, University of Wisconsin at Madison; Ann Gier, Roosevelt University; Lyle Johnson, Santa Ana College; Carolyn Duffy, St. Michael's College; Ellen Hoekstra, Henry Ford Community College; Celia Merrill, University of Texas at Austin; Ely J. Marquez, Southern Illinois U.

R.G.B.

Palo Alto, California
January 1980

CONTENTS

part 2: FOCUS ON PARAGRAPHS   79

part 1
FOCUS ON SENTENCES

INTRODUCTION: BEFORE YOU WRITE — THINK LIKE A READER

It is 1942. World War II has started. The British learn that Hitler is ready to invade England. Prime Minister Winston Churchill quickly calls a meeting of the British War Ministry.

At the time for the meeting, the ministers sit around a large table at 10 Downing Street. Suddenly the door opens. Prime Minister Churchill walks in, his face serious. Churchill stands at the head of the table. He raises his right hand in the Nazi salute. He says, "Gentlemen, I am Adolf Hitler. You are the members of the German War Council. Today we shall make final plans to invade England."

Churchill's plan worked. He wanted his statesmen to think like Germans. For the entire meeting, the statesmen thought like Germans. And in the end, the Germans did not defeat the English. Maybe thinking like Hitler helped Churchill beat Hitler.

Writers of English will also succeed better if they think like someone else. Writers need to think like their readers. By doing this, they can make their writing easier to read.

From Sentence to Paragraph will make your paragraphs easier to read by first introducing you in Part 1 to three helpful aids to *sentence* building: transitions, subordination, and parallelism. Though these may sound like big words, the ideas behind them will make your writing in English reach your reader. Then in Part 2, you will meet four *paragraph* helpers: the topic sentence, the controlling idea, unity, and coherence.

Moving from sentence-building skills in Part 1 to paragraph-building skills in Part 2, you will learn to write in a clear, well-organized way. When you have reached the end of the course, you will be communicating in written English.

Your ability to build paragraphs is the key that will open the door to a whole new world of writing competency.

1 Transitions

When a runner in a relay race passes his wand to another team member, his team keeps moving ahead. When a writer uses transitions, he keeps his ideas moving ahead.

TRANSITIONS PRE-TEST

Complete the paragraph by choosing transitions to fill in the blanks. Write the transitions on the appropriate lines below the paragraph. The first one is done for you.

Vilma likes traveling by bus better than traveling by airplane for four reasons. _____(1)_____ it costs less. She can ride by bus from New York to
(Thus, First, In fact,)
Chicago for $20. _____(2)_____, the air fare between the two cities is $78.
(And, So, Yet)
_____(3)_____, traveling by bus gives her a closer look at the cities and
(Nor, But, Second,)
countryside than she could get from a plane. _____(4)_____, she
(Still, Next, For example,)
enjoys driving through the big cities of Philadelphia, Pittsburgh, and Fort

Wayne. _____(5)_____ , Vilma finds that the passengers on the bus are
         (Third, Now, Indeed,)
often closer to her own age. _____(6)_____ , they are easy
                              (Similarly, Instead, After all, So,)
to talk with on the shared travel adventure. _____(7)_____ ,
                                              (In contrast, Finally, Otherwise,)
many airline passengers are businessmen who keep busy with
their work while flying. _____(8)_____ , riding a
                          (Therefore, Fourth, Accordingly,)
bus allows Vilma to explore any stop along the way.
_____(9)_____ , once she got off the bus at a
(On the other hand, Moreover, For instance,)
small town in Indiana and spent the night with a girl friend. ___(10)___ ,
                                                                (So, Then, Yet,)
the next day she took another bus to Chicago.
_____(11)_____ , Vilma usually prefers buses instead of
(For these reasons, At last, Now,)
planes unless she has to get somewhere in a hurry.

1. First, _____

2. _____

3. _____

4. _____

5. _____

6. _____

7. _____

8. _____

9. _____

10. _____

11. _____

Transitions are words that join one idea to another idea. Transitions add coherence to writing by joining ideas together.

Transitions add coherence in two important ways. First, transitions help *within a paragraph*. Transitions placed in sentences within a paragraph make it easier for a reader to follow the movement of an idea from one sentence to the next sentence. Second, transitions help *between paragraphs*. A transition that appears at the beginning of a paragraph carries forward the idea that was talked about in the paragraph immediately preceding.

Here is an example of transitions **within a paragraph:**

> To many foreigners, the American word *family* is confusing. Foreigners often hear an American say "My family is coming to visit." In **this** sentence, *family* means grandparents and perhaps other relatives. **However,** at other times, the same American might say, "I'm going to stay home with my family this weekend." **In this case,** he is talking about his wife and children. **This** is a much narrower meaning than the first **one.** Using *family* in **this** way makes a foreigner wonder which term *really* describes an American family. The answer, **of course,** is that there are two meanings for the word *family* in the United States — a narrow **one** and a broad **one.** And there is another term — *immediate family* — to describe something in between.

Note that there are two kinds of transitions in this paragraph. Such transitions as "however," "in this case," and "of course" are transitional words and phrases. But the pronouns "this" and "one" also act as transitions.

Now look at an example of transition **between paragraphs:**

> When an American today says "my family is coming to visit," he or she is using family in the broad sense to include cousins, uncles, grandparents, or any other relatives who do not live with him or her. That is, this person is using *family* the way it was used one hundred and fifty years ago when the majority of Americans were farmers. In that earlier time, of course, three or more generations lived under one roof — grandparents, their children, their children's spouses, and their children's children.
>
> **But** *family* is a very vague word. It can, mean for example, the speaker's parents, who do not live with him or her. Or it can mean uncles and aunts, nieces and nephews, first and second cousins, or even in-laws. As a result, the expression *immediate family* has come into use. It means something between the narrowest use of family and the broadest one: usually the grandparents, their children, and their children's children.

In this example, the transition "but" signals a change from talking about the *traditional* meaning of family in the first paragraph to talking about the *broader* meaning of family in the second paragraph. When the reader finds "but" beginning the second paragraph, the reader is prepared for the shift in the direction of thought that is coming.

The example paragraphs show transitions used at the beginning of a sentence, in the middle of a sentence, and at the end of a sentence. But not all transitions can appear in all three places. Many transitions are used only at the beginning or the middle of sentences. The placement of transitions often depends on the rhythm of a sentence or a paragraph.

Punctuating transitions may also confuse you. Rules do not help you here. A writer best learns about the position of transitions and their punctuation by practice. Study the examples in the sentences that follow.

You begin to learn about transitions by seeing how they are used in sentences. To help you organize your learning, let us divide them into ten groups. Each group is used for a different reason: (1) to explain; (2) to emphasize; (3) to qualify; (4) to illustrate; (5) to add; (6) to compare; (7) to contrast; (8) to concede; (9) to state a consequence; (10) to sum up.

TRANSITIONS THAT EXPLAIN

now, in addition, for, in this case, furthermore, in fact

1. **Now,** follow the directions carefully.
2. **In addition,** there are fifteen churches in the city.
3. **For** the president did not want to sign the bill.
4. The problem, **in this case,** is hard to solve.
5. **Furthermore,** several people telephoned the same night.
6. The meeting went on for six hours, **in fact.**

TRANSITIONS THAT EMPHASIZE

certainly, indeed, above all, surely, most important

1. **Certainly** the vaction was fun.
2. **Indeed,** a dessert is always enjoyable.
3. **Above all,** do not build an open fire in a forest.
4. **Surely** you agree that she won the debate.
5. **Most important,** the form has to be mailed by June 1.

TRANSITIONS THAT QUALIFY

but, however, although, though, yet, except for

1. **But** the clerk refused to answer.
2. The letter came two days too late, **however.**

3. We hoped, **though,** that she would change her mind.
4. **Yet** there was still a chance that he would win.
5. **Except for** one girl, all the hikers returned.

TRANSITIONS THAT ILLUSTRATE

for example, for instance, thus, such, next

1. That experiment, **for example,** was a total failure.
2. **For instance,** a telegram often costs more than a telephone call.
3. **Thus** the trip finally began.
4. **Such** an earthquake happened last year in China.
5. **Next,** think of the courses you want to take.

TRANSITIONS THAT ADD

in addition; furthermore; also; moreover; first, second, third, etc.; *then*

1. **In addition;** the tour stops in Vancouver.
2. **Furthermore,** the time for registration has been extended.
3. She **also** asked for a recent magazine.
4. They expected, **moreover,** to remodel their house.
5. **First,** you mail in an application. **Second,** you ask for an appointment. **Third,** you send them three personal references.
6. **Then** you come to a traffic light and turn right.

TRANSITIONS THAT COMPARE

like, in the same way, similarly, equally important, too

1. **Like** the owl, the fox hunts at night.
2. **In the same way,** we look for a good doctor.

3. **Similarly,** the Thais enjoy spicy foods.
4. **Equally important,** the car drives thirty miles on a gallon of gas.

TRANSITIONS THAT CONTRAST

unlike, in contrast, whereas, on the other hand, instead

1. **Unlike** the Porsche, the Cadillac is a large car.
2. **In contrast,** the red fluid does not lose its color.
3. The husband wanted a boy, **whereas** the wife wanted a girl.
4. **On the other hand,** a student needs time to relax.
5. **Instead,** the new law caused many problems.

TRANSITIONS THAT CONCEDE

although, nevertheless, of course, after all, clearly, still, yet

1. **Although** she ran after the train, it left without her.
2. He planned, **nevertheless,** to ask for a promotion.
3. It may rain tomorrow, **of course.**
4. **After all,** you learn to cook many foods in this job.
5. **Clearly,** a garden needs a lot of attention.
6. **Still,** a winter vacation can be pleasant.

TRANSITIONS THAT STATE A CONSEQUENCE

therefore, as a result, consequently, accordingly, so, otherwise.

1. They hoped, **therefore,** to pass the test.
2. **As a result,** the hospital hired three nurses.
3. **Consequently,** we opened an account at the bank.
4. **Accordingly,** she telephoned three different companies.

5. **So** the journey ended in Pittsburgh.
6. **Otherwise,** the train may leave without us.

TRANSITIONS THAT SUM UP

to sum up, finally, in conclusion, at last, in summary

1. **To sum up,** Christmas is the most important holiday.
2. **Finally,** the country agreed to issue more work permits.
3. **In conclusion,** a consulate offers more services.
4. **At last,** a treaty was signed.
5. **In summary,** recreation is big business.

Transitions work differently in English sentences than they do in the sentences of some other languages. Normally only a very long and complex English sentence contains more than a single transitional word or phrase. A writer in Chinese or Arabic, however, often uses two transitions in a sentence where a writer in English would only use one transition:

TOO MANY TRANSITIONS

Although he disagreed, **yet** he would not argue.

REVISED

Although he disagreed, he would not argue.
OR
He disagreed; **yet** he would not argue.

Pronouns as Transitions

Many of the transitions you have just studied are adverbs. These include *also, however, moreover, consequently,* and *furthermore.* But another part of speech is also used as a transition — the pronoun.

Some of the pronouns most often used as transitions are *it, they, this, that, these, those, I, he, she, they, them, such,* and *one.* When a pronoun is used as a transition, it moves a thought forward. A pronoun can appear in two places: within a sentence or linking two sentences together.

WITHIN A SENTENCE
LINKING SENTENCES

He asked what **that** meant.
We watched the hikers. **They** climbed slowly.

The following paragraph shows the pronoun *it* helping a writer to clearly present an idea:

It is the most talked-of subject in town. Every family in the community discusses **it** a half-a-dozen times a day. You mentioned **it** to at least one of your friends before you came into the room today. You think about **it** at least once during every class. **Its** passage is steady. **It** touches everyone. What is **it? It** is Time!

Synonyms as Transitions

A synonym is a word that means the same thing as another word. For example, *rich* and *wealthy* are synonyms. So are *teacher* and *instructor, trip* and *journey,* and *sick* and *ill.*

Synonyms are used as transitions in the same way that pronouns are. Synonyms move an idea forward through a paragraph or between paragraphs. Read this example of synonyms used as transitions:

Community **colleges** are like the two-year colleges called junior colleges, or "j.c.'s." Both **schools** prepare students for four-year colleges. J.c.'s offer all the courses most four-year colleges ask their freshmen and sophmores to take. Community colleges also give such required courses. But community colleges are also like other **institutions** called **trade schools.** Both schools offer **technical training.** Trade schools give courses in such areas as carpentry, nursing, television repairing, or photography. Community colleges have complete **technical courses** for students who do not plan to go on to a university.

In this paragraph, *colleges, schools, trade schools,* and *institutions* are three different ways of saying the same thing. *Technical training* and *technical courses* are also synonyms.

Coordinating Conjunctions as Transitions

The coordinating conjunctions are *and, but, for, or,* and *nor.* In informal writing (and less often in formal writing), these words can be placed as the first word in a sentence to carry over an idea from another sentence or paragraph.

Notice how coordinating conjunctions act as transitions between sentences in the following passage:

On Thursday I had to decide what I wanted to do over the weekend. **For** school was starting in two weeks, and I would soon be studying full time. I wanted to go skiing. **But** I had spent most of my money, so I couldn't travel out of town. I might go to a movie. **Or** I might just listen to music. **And** that is what I ended up doing — listening to music.

Repeating a Word for Transition

Repeating a word without meaning to repeat it makes writing dull. But repeating a word to keep an idea moving ahead helps a piece of writing. Repeating a word can add coherence. A repeated word can carry an idea from one sentence to another sentence. Or a repeated word can carry an idea from the ending of one paragraph to the beginning of the next paragraph.

How many times has the word "repeated" (or some form of it) been repeated in the paragraph you have just read? It appears twice in the first sentence and once in the following four sentences. By the time you reach the end of the paragraph, the idea of "repeating a word" has been firmly planted in your mind. Using word repetition as a transition can do the same thing for you as a writer. It can strongly reinforce an important idea that you are presenting.

Study this example of transition gained by repeating the words *gulls* and *current:*

Gulls as they soar are not always searching for food but merely having fun on the wing. A **gull** flying along the shore is taking advantage of wind **current** formed when the sea air strikes the warm land and rises. **Gulls** also love the lower, weaker air **currents** that form about three feet above the waves. They ride them for hours, tipping from one **current** to the next. Most people think that **gulls** ride behind boats for the food. But garbage is only a small part of what they eat. Clams and fish make up most of their diet. The sea **gulls** follow boats for the ride — on the thermal **currents** the ships create at sea.

TEST YOURSELF

In the two paragraphs showing transitions between paragraphs on page 7, find eight transitions. Do not include the boldfaced transition, **but,** *used between the two paragraphs.*

_____

_____

_____

Find answers to TEST YOURSELF on page 19.

FIVE WAYS TO POLISH YOUR SKILLS

Activity 1

Circle the transitions in the paragraph. Then write out the paragraph.

Life in a new country can be confusing. For example, one day I wanted to go to the consulate to renew my student visa. So my aunt gave me the consulate's address. But when I arrived downtown, I got lost. First, I went to a bank. A lady there told me to walk three blocks south. I walked three blocks north instead, however. Then I asked a policeman for help. As a result, he drove me right to the door of the consulate. From my story, you can see that I had a hard time doing one errand.

_____

_____

_____

_____

_____

_____

_____

_____

_____

_____

_____

_____

Activity 2

Choose from the list of transitions to fill in the blanks correctly in the paragraph. Then write out the paragraph.

But	Consequently	Yet
In contrast	First	Fourth
Third	Finally	Instead
Similarly	Although	Second

European universities and universities in the United States are different in many ways. _____, European students enroll in fewer courses each term than United States students do. _____, European students seldom live at a university. _____, they live at home and travel to classes. _____, most European courses are given by professors who lecture to their classes. _____, United States professors often ask their students questions or allow their students to form discussion groups. _____, European professors ask students to write fewer papers than United States professors do. _____, European students' final examinations are usually oral, whereas American students take written final examinations. _____, a European university is mainly a place to study. _____ at most United States universities, social activities take up a large part of the students' time.

_____

_____

_____

_____

_____

_____

_____

_____

_____

_____

_____

_____

_____

_____

_____

_____

_____

_____

_____

_____

_____

_____

_____

Activity 3

Write out the paragraph, adding transitions that correctly move the idea forward.

Foreign cars are often more expensive to own in the United States than American-made cars. _____, foreign cars cost more to buy. _____, there are reasons for this. The quality of workmanship that goes into making them is very high. _____ high tariffs on many foreign models have raised prices. _____, foreign cars often cost more to register. _____ insurance rates can be higher. _____, parts and repair costs are much greater than they are for American cars. _____, there are some financial advantages to owning a foreign _____, many of them get better gas mileage, and they need new tires less often than American cars do. _____, their resale value is higher. The price of a year-old foreign car may be only $300 less than what it cost new. _____ the price for a year-old American car will be around $1,000 less.

_____

_____

_____

_____

_____

_____

_____

_____

_____

_____

_____

_____

_____

_____

_____

_____

_____

_____

_____

_____

_____

Activity 4

Copy the following paragraph, adding transitions where they will improve the flow of ideas. Underline the transitions you add.

Jane and Karen have many things in common. Both girls have the same background. Jane was born and raised in the West. Karen was born and raised in the West. Both girls are interested in the same kinds of subjects in school. Jane likes French, history, and English. Karen likes Spanish, history, and English. Both girls want to be teachers. Jane plans to become an elementary school teacher. Karen wants to be a high school teacher. The two girls are almost like twins.

_____

_____

_____

_____

_____

_____

_____

_____

_____

_____

Activity 5

Copy the following paragraph, adding transitions where they will improve the flow of ideas. Underline the transitions you add.

Luis and Mario are different in three ways. Luis studies a lot. He wants to get all A's. He wouldn't get into medical school when he graduates. Mario rarely studies. He doesn't care about grades. He just wants a B.A. Luis never has time for sports. He doesn't have time to play. He sometimes watches a game. Mario spends most of his time playing soccer or basketball. Luis doesn't like parties. They usually last until two. He needs lots of sleep. Mario loves parties. He gets to bed very late. He doesn't seem to need as much sleep as Luis does. In spite of their differences, Luis and Mario are good friends.

_____

_____

_____

_____

_____

_____

_____

_____

_____

_____

_____

_____

_____

_____

_____

ANSWERS to TEST YOURSELF	That is	Or
	of course	it
	It	As a result
	for example	It

TRANSITIONS POST-TEST

Complete the paragraph by adding transitions to fill in the blanks. Write the transitions on the appropriate lines below the paragraph.

Paolo likes to fly as an airline passenger at night rather than during the day for four reasons. _____(1)_____, it costs less. _____(2)_____, he would have to pay $125 to fly from San Francisco to Mexico City by day. _____(3)_____ by night, the fare is $75. _____(4)_____, the plane is less crowded on night flights. _____(5)_____, Paolo rarely has to sit three abreast when he flies at night. _____(6)_____, he has more room to stretch out. _____(7)_____, night flights are quieter than day flights. _____(8)_____, Paolo can study or read without being distracted by loud conversations or by people walking up and down the aisle. _____(9)_____, passengers on night flights can usually sleep quite comfortably if they want to. They do _____(10)_____ by folding up the armrests between three empty seats. _____(11)_____ allows a passenger to lie down for a nap under a blanket. _____(12)_____, Paolo rarely reserves a daytime flight on a commercial airline.

1. _____
2. _____
3. _____
4. _____
5. _____
6. _____
7. _____
8. _____
9. _____
10. _____
11. _____
12. _____

2 Subordination

When people want to look especially good, they are willing to spend more than their budget allows in order to have the latest hairstyle. The least *important idea at this time — saving money — is subordinated to the* most *important idea — having attractive hair.*

When a writer wants to show a reader that one idea in a sentence is more important than another idea, the writer also subordinates the less important idea. This chapter shows you how to subordinate an idea in a sentence.

SUBORDINATION PRE-TEST

Complete each sentence by adding a subordinate clause. (A clause has a subject and a predicate.) Write out the sentence. The first one is done for you

EXAMPLE: That is _____.
                 That is **what I want to know.**

1. The man _____ was missing.
The man **who escaped from prison** was missing.

_____

2. Nobody ever tells me _____.

_____

_____

_____

3. Pay close attention _____.

_____

_____

_____

4. The lie _____ cost Raul his job.

_____

_____

_____

5. He is an example _____.

_____

_____

_____

6. The woman _____ writes mystery novels.

_____

_____

_____

7. _____, she wept with joy.

_____

_____

_____

8. The sports car driver _____ is my friend.

_____

_____

9. This year he worked harder _____

_____

_____

10. The science fiction movie _____ was entertaining.

_____

_____

11. _____ send me a postcard.

_____

_____

12. The newspaper _____ is delivered every morning.

_____

_____

13. The art gallery _____ is closed on Mondays.

_____

_____

14. The space flight _____ has been successful.

_____

_____

15. I am always wondering _____

_____

_____

The basic paragraph-building skills — the topic sentence, the controlling idea, unity, coherence, and transitions — will help you to write better in English. But one important step is still necessary. You need to become familiar with the kinds of sentences that will make your paragraphs work really well. Mastering two more techniques will give you a wide range in forming sentences. The first of these techniques is **subordination.**

What is subordination? Sometimes an idea will have two closely related parts *of different importance* that need to be placed together. A writer will want to show his reader *which* idea is the most important one. An example of this is a cause-and-effect statement (Because he was tired, he drove home.) Here, the second idea, "he drove home," is more important to the writer than the first idea, "he was tired." So "he was tired" is subordinated with the word "because." Other times, two ideas are so closely linked in action that they belong in a single sentence. An example of this is a time statement (Eve washed the dishes while her mother slept.). Here, the idea that "Eve washed the dishes" is more important than the idea "her mother slept." So "her mother slept" is subordinated with the word "while." Subordination helps you to shine a spotlight on a major idea in a sentence. At the same time, subordination helps a writer to avoid building a series of choppy, look-alike sentences that have the same grammatical structure and length.

The cartoon opening this chapter shows subordination in a real-life situation. Given two ideas — saving money and having attractive hair — the man chooses having attractive hair as his main idea. Getting a haircut at little cost becomes less important — a secondary idea.

Let us examine more closely how subordination works in these two sentences. Here you see the sentences broken into their two ideas and then joined into a single sentence with a subordinating word. The secondary idea is in italics; the subordinating word is boldfaced.

IDEA #1: He drove home. (Main idea)
IDEA #2: He was tired. (Secondary idea)
Subordinating word: **because**
IDEA #2 subordinated to IDEA #1: **Because** *he was tired*, he drove home.

OR

He drove home **because** he was tired.

IDEA #1: Eve washed the dishes. (Main idea)
IDEA #2: Her mother slept. (Secondary idea)
Subordinating word: **while**

IDEA #2 subordinated to IDEA #1: Eve washed the dishes **while** *her mother slept.*

OR

While her mother slept, Eve washed the dishes.

An idea can be subordinated in many different ways. These are the chief ways to subordinate:

1. **Subordination by an adverb clause.** You put a secondary idea in a dependent adverb clause (a clause that cannot stand alone) when you want to express the idea of time, place, cause or reason, purpose or result, or concession or contrast. These meanings are stated in the subordinating words in the following list.

TIME	Subordinating words include *before, after, when, whenever, while, until, since.*
	Patricia worked in the library **until** *it closed.* **After** *we made a picnic lunch,* we left for the beach.
PLACE	Subordinating words include *where, wherever.*
	They put a couch **where** *the chair had been.* **Wherever** *you are,* I'll find you.
CAUSE OR REASON	Subordinating words include *because, since, as, as if, as though, as long as, whereas*
	Since *you are leaving tomorrow,* we can eat dinner together tonight. She looks **as if** *she needs some more sleep.*
PURPOSE OR RESULT	Subordinating words include *that, so, so that, in order that.*
	We jogged before dinner **so that** *we would be hungry.* They carried an umbrella **in order that** *they would* stay dry in the rain.
CONCESSION OR CONTRAST	Subordinating words include *although, though, even though, unless, if, than, provided that.*

He will not be able to concentrate on his reading **unless** *you turn off the radio.*

Although *she saved money every month,* she could not afford to fly to Mexico for her vacation.

2. **Subordination by an adjective clause.** You can place a less important idea in an adjective clause beginning with *who, which,* or *that.* An adjective clause normally follows the noun or pronoun that it modifies.

Tanya was looking for someone **who** *would explain calculus to her.*

I like the dress **that** *you are wearing.*

Juan found a sleeping bag, **which** *had been left in the bus station.*

The bed **that** *you are going to make* needs clean sheets.

3. **Subordination by a modifying phrase.** A secondary idea can be subordinated by placing it in either a prepositional phrase or participial phrase. A phrase can appear at the beginning, in the middle, or at the end of a sentence.

They shopped **for** *a new stove.* (Prepositional phrase)

In *the box* she found a ruby ring. (Prepositional phrase)

Running *down the hill,* we came to a farmhouse. (Participial phrase)

Jerry stopped at the corner, **hoping to** *stop the bus.* (Participial phrase)

When a participle or participial phrase begins a sentence, a writer has to be sure that the subject of the sentence is the proper word for the participle to modify. In the following example, for instance, the participial phrase at the beginning of the sentence "Running down the hill . . ." properly modifies the subject "we." But if the sentence had been reworded so that "farmhouse" was the subject, the participial phrase would be a *dangling participle.* This is a common writing error to avoid.

Running down the hill, **we** came to a farmhouse. (Correct)

Running down the hill, **the farmhouse** came into view. (Dangling participle. This says that the farmhouse was running down the hill.)

Opening the door, **they** heard the clock strike twelve. (Correct)

Opening the door, **the clock** struck twelve. (Dangling participle. This says that the clock was opening the door.)

Captured during the evening, **the thief** was questioned by the police. (Correct)

Captured during the evening, **the police** questioned the thief. (Dangling participle. This says that the police were captured.)

4. **Subordination by an appositive.** An appositive is a word placed next to a noun, used in the same way grammatically and referring to the same person or thing. An appositive lets a writer emphasize the main idea of a sentence that contains two or more ideas. Appositives have the extra benefit of allowing a writer to use fewer words. An appositive can appear at the beginning, in the middle, or at the end of a sentence.

WEAK	The Ice Follies is an ice skating show, and it is very entertaining.
SUBORDINATED BY APPOSITIVE	**An ice skating show,** the Ice Follies is very entertaining.
WEAK	Anwar Sadat and Menachem Begin are Middle Eastern leaders, and they shared the 1978 Nobel Peace Prize.
SUBORDINATED BY APPOSITIVE	Anwar Sadat and Menachem Begin, **Middle Eastern leaders,** shared the 1978 Nobel Peace Prize.
WEAK	My father bought me a present, and it was a digital wristwatch.
SUBORDINATED BY APPOSITIVE	My father bought me a gift, **a digital wristwatch.**

TEST YOURSELF

A. *Combine each pair of sentences into a single sentence by subordinating the boldfaced idea. The first two are done for you.*

1. **The dog was chained to the fence.** He was barking noisily. *(Participial phrase)*
   Chained to the fence, the dog was barking noisily.

2. **John rented a house in London.** He planned to live in England for a year. *(Adjective clause)*
John, **who rented a home in London,** planned to live in England for a year.

3. **I opened the letter.** I read about my sister's wedding. *(Participial phrase)*

_____

_____

4. **Anthony Quinn is a Hollywood actor.** He often appears in European films. *(Appositive)*

_____

_____

5. **The bread is in the refrigerator.** It is stale. *(Prepositional phrase)*

_____

_____

6. **He wants to try a parachute jump.** He may change his mind at the last minute. *(Adverb clause)*

_____

_____

7. The dean sent me a letter. **It said I should attend summer school.** *(Adjective clause)*

_____

_____

8. **The milk bottle fell to the floor.** It broke. *(Participial phrase)*

_____

_____

_____

9. **My brother was treasurer of the company.** He was promoted to vice-president. *(Adjective clause)*

_____

_____

10. **Chicago is built along Lake Michigan.** It is known as "the windy city." *(Participial phrase)*

_____

_____

11. **I removed the tire.** Then Peter repaired the leak. *(Adverb clause)*

_____

_____

12. My aunt sent me a birthday gift. **It was a brown cashmere sweater.** *(Appositive)*

_____

_____

13. We like to eat dinner at eight o'clock. **We like lighted candles on the table.** *(Prepositional phrase)*

_____

_____

14. My parents remodeled the room. **It had been a garage.** *(Adjective clause)*

_____

_____

15. **The wedding cake had seven layers.** It was decorated by the pastry chef. *(Prepositional phrase)*

_____

_____

B. *Choose an idea in each sentence to subordinate in the way named in parentheses. The first two are done for you.*

1. I made lunch, and Alfredo washed the car. *(Adverb clause)*
   I made lunch **while Alfredo washed the car.**

2. The house is at the end of the street, and it is our dormitory. *(Prepositional phrase)*
   The house **at the end of the street** is our dormitory.

3. The airline sent us a letter, and it announced a nonstop flight to Kuala Lumpur. *(Adjective clause)*

   _____

   _____

   _____

4. Rome is the capital of Italy, and it is where the Vatican is located. *(Appositive)*

   _____

   _____

   _____

5. The river was slowly rising, and it began to overflow its banks. *(Participial phrase)*

   _____

   _____

   _____

6. You travel, and you will think of me. *(Adverb clause)*

   _____

   _____

   _____

7. We were running fast, and we caught up with the hikers. *(Participial phrase)*

   _____

   _____

   _____

8. The house has a large fireplace, and it is in the kitchen. *(Prepositional phrase)*

_____

_____

_____

9. It is late, and he has to leave now. *(Adverb clause)*

_____

_____

_____

10. Romola has six older brothers and sisters, and she has never gone to college. *(Adjective clause)*

_____

_____

_____

11. We were waiting for the train to arrive, and we read our books. *(Participial phrase)*

_____

_____

_____

12. Eleanora Duse was a famous actress, and she had only one leg. *(Appositive)*

_____

_____

_____

13. The geyser called Old Faithful is in Yellowstone National Park, and it is exciting to see. *(Prepositional phrase)*

_____

_____

_____

14. She wrapped the package as quickly as she could, but the post office was closed when she reached it. *(Adverb clause)*

_____

_____

_____

15. The magazine published a special anniversary edition, and it was mailed to all subscribers. *(Adjective clause)*

_____

_____

_____

Find answers to TEST YOURSELF on page 42.

FOUR WAYS TO POLISH YOUR SKILLS

Activity 6

On the lines after each number, write the main clause from the sentence on the first line. Then replace the boldfaced dependent clause or phrase by adding a new one. The first two are done for you.

1. The most important building **that I have found** is the post office.
   The most important building **in town** is the post office.

2. I go to the post office to pick up my mail **from general delivery.**
   I go to the post office to pick up my mail **after work.**

3. At the post office, I buy stamps **for my letters.**

_____

_____

_____

4. **When I have a package to mail,** I go to the post office.

_____

_____

_____

5. The post office is a good place to go **when you want to send money through the mail safely.**

_____

_____

_____

6. You can buy a money order **at the post office.**

_____

_____

_____

7. **If I find that I need state or federal income tax forms,** the post office will help me.

_____

_____

_____

8. People **who need to apply for a passport** can visit the post office.

_____

_____

_____

9. **Before I had a mailing address,** I rented a post office box.

_____

_____

_____

10. I could open my post office box **at any time of day or night.**

_____

_____

_____

11. At the post office you can get **envelopes with stamps printed on them.**

_____

_____

_____

12. **If you are a stamp collector,** one window at the post office sells special issue stamps.

_____

_____

_____

13. The bulletin board at the post office contains notices **of examinations for federal jobs.**

_____

_____

_____

14. **If the post office is closed,** you can buy stamps from a stamp machine in the lobby.

_____

_____

_____

15. I think I visit the post office more often **than I go to the bank.**

Activity 7

Add main clauses to these subordinate clauses and phrases to form complete sentences. The first two are done for you.

1. because I was too busy
   I didn't go to the movie because I was too busy.

2. who opened the door
   The woman who opened the door **was very friendly.**

3. before she left for school

_____

_____

_____

4. walking up the hill

_____

_____

_____

5. at the counter

_____

_____

6. the lifeguard at the swimming pool

_____

_____

_____

7. reading quietly

_____

_____

_____

8. unless you want to

_____

_____

_____

9. in the backyard

_____

_____

_____

10. who telephoned you

_____

_____

_____

11. until I return home

_____

_____

_____

12. a famous athlete

_____

_____

_____

13. on the bulletin board

_____

_____

_____

14. who works for a department store

_____

_____

_____

15. to the fish market

_____

_____

_____

Activity 8

Add subordinate clauses and phrases to expand these main clauses. Add the kinds of clause or phrase named in parentheses. The first two are done for you.

1. The woman is blonde. *(Adjective clause)*
   The woman **who is sitting at the table** *is blonde.*

2. The man is tall. *(Prepositional phrase)*
   The man **by the window** is tall.

3. The house is comfortable. *(Adverb clause)*

   _____

   _____

   _____

4. The building is a skyscraper. *(Appositive)*

   _____

   _____

   _____

5. The airplane is a Boeing 727. *(Prepositional phrase)*

_____

_____

_____

6. The chair is an antique. *(Adjective clause)*

_____

_____

_____

7. The car is the latest model. *(Adjective clause)*

_____

_____

_____

8. The college is coeducational. *(Adjective clause)*

_____

_____

_____

9. The grass is green. *(Adverb clause)*

_____

_____

_____

10. The ocean is very warm. *(Prepositional phrase)*

_____

_____

_____

11. The child is laughing. *(Participial phrase)*

_____

_____

_____

12. I go backpacking. *(Prepositional phrase)*

_____

_____

_____

13. The clouds become dark. *(Adverb clause)*

_____

_____

_____

14. The kitten is playing. *(Prepositional phrase)*

_____

_____

_____

15. The wind is blowing. *(Prepositional phrase)*

_____

_____

_____

Activity 9

Choose two words from each group. For each of the twelve words you choose, write a sentence that contains the word, a main clause, and a subordinate clause. The first two are done for you.

Time Adverbs	*Place Adverbs*	*Cause Adverbs*
before	where	because
after	wherever	since
when		as
whenever		as if
while		as though
until		as long as
since		whereas

Purpose Adverbs	*Concession Adverbs*	*Relative Pronouns*
that	although	who
so	though	which

so that   even though   that
in order that   unless
                            if
                            than
                            provided that

1. before
   Before I go shopping, I make out a shopping list.
2. as if
   She looks **as if** someone has told her a secret.

3. _____

_____

_____

4. _____

_____

_____

5. _____

_____

_____

6. _____

_____

_____

7. _____

_____

_____

8. _____

_____

_____

9. _____

_____

_____

10. _____

_____

_____

11. _____

_____

_____

12. _____

_____

_____

13. _____

_____

_____

14. _____

_____

_____

ANSWERS to TEST YOURSELF

A. 3. Opening the letter, I read about my sister's wedding.
    4. Anthony Quinn, a Hollywood actor, often appears in European films.
    5. The bread in the refrigerator is stale
    6. Although he wants to try a parachute jump, he may change his mind at the last minute.
    7. The dean sent me a letter that said I should attend summer school.
    8. Falling to the floor, the milk bottle broke.
    9. My brother, who was treasurer of the company, was promoted to vice-president.
   10. Chicago, built along Lake Michigan, is known as "the windy city."
   11. After I removed the tire, Peter repaired the leak.
   12. My aunt sent me a birthday gift, a brown cashmere sweater.
   13. We like to eat dinner at eight o'clock with lighted candles on the table.
   14. My parents remodeled the room that had been a garage.
   15. The wedding cake with seven layers was decorated by the pastry chef.
B. 3. The airline sent us a letter that announced a nonstop flight to Kuala Lumpur.
    4. Rome, the capital of Italy, is where the Vatican is located.

5. Slowly rising, the river began to overflow its banks.
6. Wherever you travel, you will think of me.
7. Running fast, we caught up with the hikers.
8. The house has a large fireplace in the kitchen.
9. Because it is late, he has to leave now.
10. Romola, who has six other brothers and sisters, has never gone to college.
11. Waiting for the train to arrive, we read our books.
12. Eleanora Duse, a famous actress, had only one leg.
13. The geyser called Old Faithful in Yellowstone National Park is exciting to see.
14. Although she wrapped the package as quickly as she could, the post office was closed when she reached there.
15. The magazine published a special anniversary edition that was mailed to all subscribers.

SUBORDINATION POST-TEST

Add a subordinate clause to expand each of these short sentences.

EXAMPLE: The safe is locked.
            The safe **where the jewels are kept** is locked.

1. The door is open.

   _____

   _____

   _____

2. We are walking.

   _____

   _____

   _____

3. The woman is well-dressed.

   _____

   _____

   _____

4. Sergio is driving.

   _____

   _____

   _____

5. The time has come.

   _____

   _____

   _____

6. The concert begins at 8:30 P.M.

   _____

   _____

   _____

   _____

   _____

7. The airplane is taking off.

_____

_____

_____

8. The dog is a German shepherd.

_____

_____

_____

9. That car has a turbo engine.

_____

_____

_____

10. This book is interesting.

_____

_____

_____

11. The actress won an award.

_____

_____

_____

12. The lamp is new.

_____

_____

_____

13. The boat sails tomorrow.

_____

_____

_____

14. Those sunglasses are his.

_____

_____

_____

15. These packages are gifts.

_____

_____

_____

③ PARALLELISM

To become a good skier, a person learns how to keep skis on parallel tracks while speeding down a slope. Parallel structure in writing also makes it possible for a writer to move forward smoothly.

PARALLELISM PRE-TEST

Write the parallel elements that appear in each sentence on the line under the sentence. The first one is done for you.

EXAMPLE: I told her about the woman who asked for directions and who gave us a candy bar.

who asked for directions
who gave us a candy bar

1. Camila spends most of her time reading and cooking.

_____

_____

_____

2. Steve needs to explore his goals and to decide about his future.

_____

_____

_____

3. My paycheck shows deductions for federal income tax, state income tax, and Social Security.

_____

_____

_____

4. We went through the front door and up the stairs to reach Mr. Martin's office.

_____

_____

_____

5. His favorite hobbies are to build model airplanes and to collect stamps.

_____

_____

_____

6. Tana wants to learn how to write a check and how to deposit money in the bank.

_____

_____

_____

7. The travel agent asked us when we planned to leave and what stops we would like to make.

_____

_____

_____

8. To play chess and to play backgammon are two of my favorite recreations.

_____

9. Many cities provide bicyclists with both bicycle lanes and bicycle racks.

10. You can shop for a car in the classified pages of a newspaper, in a used car lot, or in a new car showroom.

11. If I can't telephone you from home, I will phone you from a telephone booth.

12. After Tom proposed marriage and gave Colleen a ring, she could not wait to tell her family.

13. Typing and taking shorthand are two requirements for a secretarial job.

14. Nothing he has said has shown me that he either wants to study or cares about graduating.

15. Helen thought about leaving the dining room and running up to her bedroom.

_____

_____

_____

Parallelism (or parallel structure) can be explained in both a general and a specific way. Generally speaking, parallelism is a writer's method of expressing similar ideas in similar grammatical forms. Specifically, parallel structure means keeping parts of a sentence grammatically the same when they are in a series or when they are joined by correlative conjunctions.

PARALLELISM IN A SERIES	They had their choice of **watching** television, **going** shopping, or **eating** out.
PARALLELISM WITH CORRELATIVE CONJUNCTIONS	He is _both_ a good **pitcher** _and_ a good **hitter** for the baseball team.

Parallelism is the writer's technique of balancing like with like — nouns with nouns, verbs with verbs, infinitives with infinitives, prepositional phrases with prepositional phrases, and so forth.

Before understanding parallelism, a student might ask: "Why is parallelism important to a writer?" After studying parallelism, the student will find that parallel structure helps to present ideas to a reader in the clearest possible way. In many ways, parallelism also serves the function of transition, carrying the reader easily along from one idea to the next.

Almost any kind of sentence element can appear in a parallel form:

SINGLE WORDS	**India, Bali,** and **East Africa** are my favorite travel destinations. _(Nouns)._
	Andreas **skis, bowls,** and **surfs.** _(Verbs)_
	Her fiancé was **witty, intelligent,** and **experienced.** _(Adjectives)_
	The horse jumped **quickly** and **surely** over the rail fence. _(Adverbs)_
	We spent the day **swimming, reading,** and **sleeping.** _(Participles)_

PHRASES   They searched for the books **in the living room, in the bedroom,** and **in the garage.** *(Prepositional phrases)*
To finish school *and* **to get a good job** are my ambitions. *(Infinitive phrases)*
I spent my time in the train compartment **eating my lunch** and **talking with the other passengers.** *(Participial phrases)*
Filling out the marriage license and **signing it** were the last steps. *(Gerund phrases)*

CLAUSES   They are looking for a house **that has four bedrooms** and **that sits on a hillside lot.** *(Adjective clauses)*
If you leave a note or **if you telephone,** I will get your message. *(Adverb clauses)*

Parallel structure breaks down when elements that are similar in idea are not kept similar in structure. Here are typical examples of faulty parallelism, with revisions to make the elements parallel:

FAULTY   She likes **to knit, to sew,** and **crocheting.**
REVISED   She likes **to knit, to sew,** and **to crochet.**

FAULTY   The doctor suggested plenty of **food, rest,** and **exercising.**
REVISED   The doctor suggested plenty of **food, rest,** and **exercise.**

FAULTY   Come to class prepared **to take** notes and **with some questions** to ask.
REVISED   Come to class prepared **to take notes** and **to ask some questions.**

FAULTY   He is good not only **at hockey** but **plays basketball** well too.
REVISED   He is good not only **at hockey** but also **at basketball.**

FAULTY   The award was for a combination of **scholarship, someone who was a good leader,** and **ability in athletics.**
REVISED   The award was for a combination of **scholarship, leadership,** and **athletic ability.**

FAULTY	I forgot **that the bill was due** on Monday and **the company would close my account** if it wasn't paid.
REVISED	I forgot **that the bill was due** on Monday and **that the company would close my account** if it wasn't paid.

Faulty parallelism can often be corrected in more than one way:

FAULTY	**To drive** well and **staying** within the speed limits are necessary in today's traffic.
REVISED	**To drive** well and **to stay** within the speed limits are necessary in today's traffic. *(Both infinitive phrases)*

OR

REVISED	**Driving** well and **staying** within the speed limits are necessary in today's traffic. *(Both participial phrases)*

In a series the parts of the first item that are repeated in the second item must be repeated in all the other items as well. But unnecessary items may be dropped from the second item and therefore from all other items. This is especially true when the same pronoun, preposition, or article would otherwise have to be repeated several times:

UNNECESSARY REPETITION	The Olympic runner was praised **for his** strength and **for his** endurance.
REVISED	The Olympic runner was praised for his strength and endurance.
UNNECESSARY REPETITION	We installed wood paneling **in the** living room, **in the** dining room, and **in the** kitchen.
REVISED	We installed wood paneling in the living room, dining room, and kitchen.

But do not leave out elements needed for clarity:

UNCLEAR	At the conference Laura met a doctor, writer, and world traveler. *(Is the doctor, writer, and world traveler one person or three separate people?)*
REVISED	At the conference Laura met a man who was a doctor, writer, and world traveler. *(One person)*

OR

At the conference Laura met a doctor, a writer, and a world traveler. *(Three separate people)*

UNCLEAR   The man denied that he had broken into the house and he had taken the watch.

REVISED   The man denied **that** he had broken into the house and **that** he had taken the watch.

OR

REVISED   The man denied that he had broken into the house and taken the watch.

UNCLEAR   The hurricane was more of a threat to the tourists than the natives.

REVISED   The hurricane was more of a threat **to** the tourists than **to** the natives.

Besides adding the qualities of clarity and coherence to writing, parallelism can also help a writer to build a climatic order of ideas. (Sentences and paragraphs are strongest when they build to a climax, just as television shows and motion pictures do.) Parallelism can be used to create a climactic build with words, phrases, clauses, or whole sentences:

WORDS   I value a friend who is **sweet, kind,** and **loving.**

PHRASES   We drove first **to the lake,** then **to the river,** and finally **to the ocean.**

CLAUSES   She had the same feeling **when she graduated from middle school, when she graduated from high school,** and **when she graduated from college.**

SENTENCES   Never had Brent seen such chaos as during the earthquake. **Windows of storefronts were shattering. Streets were splitting open. Bricks and boulders were crashing down from tall buildings on the people below.**

TEST YOURSELF

A. *Revise these sentences to make the elements in them parallel.*

EXAMPLE: Knowing how to study and to learn to budget time are important for college students.
Knowing how to study and **learning how to budget time** are important for college students.

1. Leonardo da Vinci was known both as an inventor and painting pictres.

_____

_____

_____

2. Shirley has been a waitress, a tour guide, and taught school.

_____

_____

_____

3. To swim in a pool is not as much fun as swimming in a river.

_____

_____

_____

4. Dentists advise brushing your teeth after every meal and to avoid sugar in your diet.

_____

_____

_____

5. My orders said that I was assigned to Alaska and I should leave within two weeks.

_____

_____

_____

6. We asked the store manager to show us a gift that was inexpensive, useful, and looked nice.

_____

_____

_____

7. The hotel clerk knew that we had paid our bill and we had our receipt.

_____

_____

_____

8. My uncle spoke with warmth and in a humorous way.

_____

_____

_____

9. Our instructor suggested several books for supplementary reading and that we should do research on the subject.

_____

_____

_____

10. Several people were caught in the hailstorm but not being seriously hurt.

_____

_____

_____

11. We met a Frenchman who had lived in Brazil, but he knew very little about his own country.

_____

_____

12. Alberto was away for ten years before he was able to return home and saw his family.

_____

_____

_____

13. The boy who came to our house asked to be fed and where he could be clothed.

_____

_____

_____

14. For me, listening to FM radio is more enjoyable than to listen to AM radio.

_____

_____

_____

15. My friend's father is a good man who is kind.

_____

_____

_____

B. _Add one parallel element to each pair or words or phrases to form a series. Then write a sentence that includes the series._

EXAMPLE: scrambled eggs/toast
            scrambled eggs/toast/**coffee**
            I like scrambled eggs, toast, and **coffee** for breakfast.

1. hunts/fishes

_____

_____

_____

2. greedy/selfish

_____

_____

_____

3. neatly/prettily

_____

_____

_____

4. in the morning/in the afternoon

_____

_____

_____

5. sew/cook

_____

_____

_____

6. to travel/to photograph

_____

_____

_____

7. building a campfire/cleaning the fish *(Use as participial phrases)*

_____

_____

_____

8. reading from a menu/ordering the right meal *(Use as gerund phrases)*

_____

_____

_____

9. who took our photograph/who gave us a balloon

_____

_____

_____

10. if you arrive on time/if you will be late

_____

_____

_____

11. roller skating/watching a Walt Disney movie *(Use as participial phrases)*

_____

_____

_____

12. library/post office

_____

_____

_____

13. at a nightclub/at a discotheque

_____

_____

_____

14. renewing my student visa/taking a driving test *(Use as participial phrases)*

_____

_____

_____

15. riding the subway/going to a museum *(Use as gerund phrases)*

_____

_____

_____

Find answers to TEST YOURSELF on page 73.

FIVE WAYS TO POLISH YOUR SKILLS

Activity 10

Complete each sentence with a parallel form. Then write out the completed sentence.

EXAMPLE: I went to private schools in Switzerland and _____.
            I went to private schools in Switzerland and **France.**

1. Hang gliding and _____ are sports I would like to try.

_____

_____

_____

2. I like to read science fiction and _____ books.

_____

_____

_____

3. We lit candles in the kitchen and _____.

_____

_____

_____

4. Sicily, Rhodes, and _____ are islands.

_____

_____

_____

5. Jogging for three miles and _____ are good forms of exercise.

_____

_____

_____

6. Jaime scuba dives and _____ in Hawaii.

_____

_____

_____

7. My brother is talented musically and _____.

_____

_____

_____

8. Attending the Mardi Gras and _____ are two reasons for visiting New Orleans.

_____

_____

_____

9. They shared a picnic lunch and _____ in the park.

_____

_____

_____

10. Her sister is bright, pretty, and _____.

_____

_____

_____

11. Walking to school and _____ are my biggest problems.

_____

_____

_____

12. Sarah looked at a studio apartment and _____.

_____

_____

_____

13. We want a car that has disc brakes and _____.

_____

_____

_____

14. To write a novel and _____ are my goals.

_____

_____

_____

15. When you find a dress you like and _____, let me know.

_____

_____

_____

Activity 11

First make each pair of elements parallel. Then write a sentence that correctly includes the rewritten elements.

EXAMPLE: the hardware store/shopping for groceries
the hardware store/**the grocery store**
We have errands to do at **the hardware store** and the **grocery store.**

1. repair the old house/building a new one

_____

_____

_____

2. star football player/studies well

_____

_____

_____

3. reads newspaper advertisements/shopping for clothing

_____

_____

_____

4. buying a bus ticket/boarded the bus

_____

_____

_____

5. plays unfairly/poor loser

_____

_____

_____

6. installing stereo speakers/water hanging plants

_____

_____

_____

7. inquire about a loan/filling out forms

_____

_____

_____

8. a raise in salary/moved to another city

_____

_____

_____

9. intelligent/eager to succeed in his studies

_____

_____

_____

10. ride a moped/bicycling

_____

_____

_____

11. successful teacher/coaches sports well

_____

_____

_____

12. employment agency/eating lunch

_____

_____

_____

13. to a laundromat/getting a haircut

_____

_____

_____

14. flagged down a taxicab/asking what the fare would be

_____

_____

_____

15. ordering a Eurailpass/bought airline tickets

_____

_____

_____

Activity 12

Add parallel elements after each of these pairs of correlative conjunctions. Then write them out in complete sentences.

EXAMPLE: either/or
            I want to go either **hiking** or **horseback riding.**

1. either/or

_____

_____

_____

2. either/or

_____

_____

_____

3. neither/nor

_____

_____

_____

4. neither/nor

_____

_____

_____

5. not only/but also

_____

_____

_____

6. not only/but also

_____

_____

_____

7. both/and

_____

_____

_____

8. both/and

_____

_____

_____

9. whether/or

_____

_____

_____

10. whether/or

_____

_____

_____

11. although/yet

_____

_____

_____

12. though/yet

_____

_____

_____

13. if/then

_____

_____

_____

14. either/or

_____

_____

_____

15. not only/but also

_____

_____

_____

Activity 13

Write original sentences that contain these grammatical elements in parallel forms.

EXAMPLE: adverbs
            She walked **sadly** and **quietly** out of the room.

1. nouns

_____

_____

_____

2. nouns

_____

_____

_____

3. verbs

_____

_____

_____

4. verbs

_____

_____

_____

5. adjectives

_____

_____

6. adjectives

_____

_____

7. adverbs

_____

_____

8. adverbs

_____

_____

9. participles

_____

_____

10. participles

_____

_____

11. prepositional phrases

_____

_____

_____

5. _____

_____

_____

_____

6. _____

_____

_____

_____

7. _____

_____

_____

_____

8. _____

_____

_____

_____

9. _____

_____

_____

_____

10. _____

_____

_____

_____

11. _____

_____

_____

_____

_____

5. adjectives

_____

_____

6. adjectives

_____

_____

7. adverbs

_____

_____

8. adverbs

_____

_____

9. participles

_____

_____

10. participles

_____

_____

11. prepositional phrases

_____

_____

_____

12. prepositional phrases

_____

_____

13. infinitive phrases

_____

_____

14. infinitive phrases

_____

_____

15. participial phrases

_____

_____

16. participial phrases

_____

_____

17. adjective clauses

_____

_____

18. adjective clauses

_____

_____

_____

19. adverb clauses

_____

_____

_____

20. adverb clauses

_____

_____

_____

Activity 14

Find fifteen examples of parallel structure in sentences in the chapters of this book. Write out the examples in the spaces below.

1. _____

_____

_____

_____

2. _____

_____

_____

_____

3. _____

_____

_____

_____

4. _____

_____

5. _____

6. _____

7. _____

8. _____

9. _____

10. _____

11. _____

12. _____

_____

_____

_____

13. _____

_____

_____

14. _____

_____

_____

15. _____

_____

_____

_____

ANSWERS to TEST YOURSELF

A.   1. Leonardo da Vinci was known both as an inventor and painter.
   2. Shirley has been a waitress, tour guide, and schoolteacher.
   3. To swim in a pool is not as much fun as to swim in a river.
   4. Dentists advise brushing your teeth after every meal and avoiding sugar in your diet.
   5. My orders said that I was assigned to Alaska and that I should leave within two weeks.
   6. We asked the store manager for a gift that was inexpensive, useful, and beautiful.
   7. The hotel clerk knew that we had paid our bill and that we had our receipt.
   8. My uncle spoke with warmth and humor.
   9. Our instructor suggested that we should read several supplementary books and that we should do research in the library.

10. Several people were caught in the hailstorm but were not seriously hurt.
11. We met a Frenchman who lived in Brazil but who knew very little about his own country.
12. Alberto was away for ten years before he was able to return home and see his family.
13. The boy who came to our house asked to be fed and clothed.
14. For me, listening to FM radio is more enjoyable than listening to AM radio.
15. My friend's father is a good and kind man.

B. (Possible student answers)
1. My brother hunts, fishes, and climbs mountains.
2. I stay away from people who are greedy, selfish, and unpleasant to be with.
3. The store wrapped the package neatly, prettily, and quickly.
4. She studied in the morning, in the afternoon, and in the evening.
5. My mother was looking for someone to sew, cook, and clean.
6. He likes to travel, to photograph, and to collect coins.
7. Gail spent her time building a campfire, cleaning the fish, and cooking it.
8. Reading from a menu, ordering the right meal, and having enough money to pay for it is an art.
9. The man who was wearing old clothes, who took our photograph, and who gave us a balloon has left the park.
10. Let me know if you are on time, if you will be late, or if you decide not to come.
11. We decided to spend Friday night roller skating, watching a Walt Disney movie, and eating a midnight snack.
12. Esther made stops at the library, post office, and bank.
13. On weekends we like to meet our friends at a nightclub, at a discotheque, and at a roller derby.
14. Yesterday I spent all day renewing my student visa, taking my driving test, and going to the dentist.
15. Riding the subway, going to a museum, and exploring Greenwich Village was our plan for Sunday.

PARALLELISM POST-TEST

Correct the faulty parallelism in these sentences by rewriting the sentences correctly. Underline the corrected parallel element.

EXAMPLE: He enjoys walking, jogging, and to ride a bicycle.
                  He enjoys walking, jogging, and **riding** a bicycle.

1. She was eating her sandwich and drank her milk at the table when I arrived.

   _____

   _____

   _____

2. We came across a cave that looked like a safe resting place and that was comfortable.

   _____

   _____

   _____

3. When father came home with his boss and finds the house a mess, he was angry.

   _____

   _____

   _____

4. Gloria knew that patience, calmness, and if she was affectionate would quiet the child down.

   _____

   _____

   _____

5. David killed the snake with a big branch that he had cut from a tree and which was whittled to a sharp point.

   _____

   _____

   _____

   _____

6. After the automobile crash, Anne lay in the back seat, in a state of pain and being shocked.

_____

_____

_____

7. They hiked for two days and during two nights until they reached the mountaintop.

_____

_____

_____

8. Tim had expected a negative vote and a plan was in his mind to work around it.

_____

_____

_____

9. We seated ourselves in the airplane, not in the first-class compartment but where tourist passengers sit.

_____

_____

_____

10. The dean is a man of intelligence, humor, and one who is wise.

_____

_____

_____

11. They gave Andrea the award for the best essay, honoring her and which made her feel proud.

_____

_____

_____

12. Claude was nervous and feeling annoyance because he had lost his keys.

_____

_____

_____

13. It took the Green warrior hero Ulysses ten years of wandering and he suffered to reach his home.

_____

_____

14. Soon Consuela stopped worrying and she was developing a brighter outlook on life.

_____

_____

15. Dorothy had to learn not only how to find a job but also keeping a job.

_____

_____

_____

part 2
FOCUS ON PARAGRAPHS

PARAGRAPH WRITING PRE-TEST

1. Choose one of these topic sentences as the first sentence of a paragraph you write. Circle the word or words that state the controlling (or central) idea of the paragraph. Your paragraph should contain at least six sentences.

   1. A visit to a foreign country is always filled with surprises.
   2. It is not easy to find the right kind of off-campus housing.
   3. For some reason, many of the classes I want to take meet at the same hour on the same days.
   4. The university has a certain method of assigning roommates.
   5. Weekends mean different things to different people.

_____

_____

_____

_____

_____

_____

_____

_____

_____

_____

_____

_____

_____

_____

_____

_____

_____

_____

_____

_____

2. Think up a topic sentence with a controlling idea on a subject that interests you. Then develop a paragraph of at least eight sentences based on your topic sentence.

_____

_____

_____

_____

_____

_____

_____

_____

_____

_____

_____

_____

_____

_____

_____

_____

_____

_____

_____

_____

_____

_____

_____

_____

FOUR PRE-WRITING STEPS

Experienced writers know that pre-writing is just as important as writing itself. But what is pre-writing? How can students learn this professional way to improve their paragraph writing? The four pre-writing steps are (1) Choosing a Topic, (2) Narrowing a Topic, (3) Outlining Your Ideas, and (4) Forming a Topic Sentence.

In the following pages, you will find an explanation of the four pre-writing steps. This information is more than an introduction to this book. It gives you material that can be used to produce better paragraphs every time you write.

STEP 1: Choosing a Topic

Although an instructor will often assign a topic to students, there are occasions when a student will have to choose a topic. When this happens, selecting a topic to write about can be a big problem. Some students may feel that no one would be interested in what they have to say on any subject. Others may be too shy to put their real thoughts or feelings down on paper.

One rule can help *any* student select a topic to write about: *Always write about a subject you know very well.* The hardest writing job comes when a writer is struggling with unfamiliar material.

Even though the subjects you know a lot about may not seem to you to be good topics, that should not stop you. If you choose a topic that really interests you, your reader will respond to the fact that you really know what you are writing about. Your interest in your topic will shine through your written words.

Any topic — no matter how minor — can be brought to life if a writer really knows the subject matter. There is a ready audience for every possible topic. One person might like to read about how to baby-sit, another person might like to read about how to find an apartment, and still another person might want to learn how to start a pedicab business in Honolulu. Just think how many readers would like to find out how to make sure that they get a good night's sleep. Nothing is too simple, or too specialized, to write about — as long as you know your subject well.

To begin your thinking on the choice of a subject, turn to the list of composition topics in Appendix 2. Read these topics over and place checks by the topics you feel you know enough about and like well enough to use as the basis for developing a paragraph.

Next, practice choosing a topic in your own mind. Think over the subjects that really interest you. Then make a short list of possible topics.

Cross off the topics that seem too limited for you to develop well. Then choose the topic that seems the most promising. Test the topic by making sure that it breaks into enough parts to include in a paragraph.

Finally, write out your best topic here:

_____

STEP 2: Narrowing a Topic

Once you have chosen a topic that you feel confident about, the next pre-writing step is to narrow the subject down to a small, workable unit. The secret of successful writing is to select *that part of a subject* which you can develop most effectively. If you do not take this important narrowing step, you could be faced with a subject that is much too large to handle in a single paragraph.

Let us look at two cases of writers narrowing their topics. Suppose a student decides that automobiles is a good topic. Because the student is interested in automobiles and knows a lot about them, this is probably a wise choice. But now comes the need to narrow this very broad topic. The subject of automobiles could be broken down into dozens of different smaller parts. Will the student write about all the new features of this year's models? Will the student write about the differences between domestic and foreign-made cars? About all of the engine options that can be ordered? About engineering advances in automobiles? Clearly, the student has to think through the many parts of this wide-ranging subject until a part can be found with which the student is comfortable.

When a student realizes the need to take a small bite of a broad subject, the question remains: "What will the bite be?" Because this student knows a lot about automobile engines, the topic can be narrowed down to a small but significant part of the subject of automobiles: the differences between internal combustion and diesel engines.

Now consider another student's similar problem of narrowing a topic from the general subject of cooking. There are many possibilities for writing: different cultural cuisines, time-saving cooking implements, great chefs of the world, famous dishes named after celebrities. The clever student tries to think of as many parts of the subject of cooking as possible. Doing this leads to the choice of a topic the student feels able to write about — cooking an omelet.

Every time you select a subject to write about, be sure to take this same narrowing approach. Break the subject into as many small topics as you can. One of these topics will be the basis for a very good paragraph. Narrowing down your subject is a vital step to take before you write a single word.

STEP 3: Outlining Your Ideas

Now that you have narrowed your topic, the next pre-writing stage is to make some kind of outline of your ideas. This procedure has several advantages. First, it lets you record all your thoughts so that none of them slips away later when it is time to write. Second, outlining the ideas you will write about in your paragraph will suggest the best way to organize the paragraph. Seeing the ideas jotted down on paper may show you that what you thought should be placed first really belongs in the middle or at the end of the paragraph.

To see how well outlining works, study the outlines that students might have written for the two narrowed-down topics that were discussed in the previous section.

The student writing about internal combustion and diesel engines might put together this kind of outline:

Diesel Engine

1. Diesel fuel costs less.
2. Fewer moving parts to repair.
3. Status value.

Internal Combustion Engine

1. Less expensive initial cost than diesel.
2. Quieter running than diesel.
3. More economy at less than 20,000 miles of driving a year.

After seeing the ideas written out, the student might want to change the order of discussing the engines. The student might decide that it would be better to talk about the more familiar engine — the internal combustion engine — first before writing about the less familiar diesel engine. So when writing begins, the student may reverse the order of the engines first set down in the outline.

This kind of helpful pre-planning can only happen when you make outline notes — even very rough ones — before you write. Outlining is an easy way to write the first draft of a paragraph. Certainly it is a sure way to produce a more polished final paragraph.

Now look at the outline notes made by the student writing about cooking an omelet:

Making an Omelet

1. Use warm eggs.
2. Beat eggs lightly with a fork.
3. Season with salt and pepper.
4. Grease the pan with butter or olive oil.
5. Cook on a low heat.
6. Add a small amount of water, not milk.
7. Turn the omelet by flipping it in the pan.
8. Do not overcook the omelet.

By reviewing these eight outlined ideas, the student might realize that one point (#6) is out of order. So the student would move #6 up to be the third point, fitting it in after "Beat eggs lightly with a fork." Notice how much easier it is to make corrections like this in a brief outline than it would be in a finished paragraph.

STEP 4: Forming a Topic Sentence

The last step to take before writing is to formulate an effective topic sentence. This sentence should tell your reader exactly what you are going to write about. It should introduce the paragraph's main idea.

Once you have taken the earlier three pre-writing steps, it is easy to form a topic sentence. Simply think back to your narrowed-down topic; this topic is what you should present in your topic sentence. A topic sentence is a limited assertion. It limits itself to the narrowed-down topic, and it asserts (or states) only that.

Let us practice forming topic sentences for the two paragraphs we have seen outlined in the last section — one on automobile engines, the other on omelets. In the case of the engines, the narrowing-down process focused on the two types of engines, internal combustion and diesel. Studying the writer's outline shows that the *advantages* of the two kinds of engine will be written about. A fitting topic sentence to open the paragraph might be this: "Internal combustion and diesel automobile engines each offer advantages to a driver."

We can check this topic sentence against the outline again to make sure that the topic sentence accurately reflects the ideas stated in the outline. Note that, in this topic sentence, the controlling (or central) idea is expressed in the single word "advantages." In every topic sentence, the central idea of the paragraph should be stated in one or more words. This controlling idea helps a reader to see quickly what information a paragraph will contain. A controlling idea also helps keep a writer from straying from the subject in writing a paragraph.

In the case of the paragraph on omelet making, the idea of cooking an omelet also came from the narrowing-down process. Looking at the outline, the writer sees that eight steps are listed. So an accurate topic sentence might be: "There are eight steps to follow in cooking a successful omelet."

The controlling idea of this topic sentence is found in the words "eight steps." These eight steps are what the writer will follow in composing the paragraph.

4 TOPIC SENTENCE

If you aim a Frisbee well, your partner will be able to catch it more easily. And if a writer puts a topic sentence in a paragraph, a reader will be more likely to catch the paragraph's main idea.

TOPIC SENTENCE PRE-TEST

1. Write out the paragraph's topic sentence on the lines below the paragraph. (A topic sentence tells the main idea of a paragraph.)

Over the past one hundred years, many North Americans have moved from the country to the city. In recent years, people have moved to the suburbs of cities. These moves have caused North American customs to change. One major change has been in shopping habits. Farmers, city dwellers, and suburbanites all have their own special approaches to buying things. Depending on where they live and the kind of shops available to them, North Americans today have three different ways of buying what they need.

_____

_____

---

2. Look at the cartoons at the beginning of Chapters 4, 5, and 6. On the lines below, write a sentence telling the main idea you see in each cartoon.

Chapter 4: _____

_____

_____

Chapter 5: _____

_____

_____

Chapter 6: _____

_____

_____

Reading a book is like driving an automobile along a highway. Why? Both a driver and a reader try to learn where they are going before they start out. Drivers learn where they are going by looking at road maps. Readers learn where they are going by looking at the title of a chapter or composition.

But when a driver and a reader begin to move ahead, they need help. They need signs to point them toward the right direction. Highway signs direct drivers; they tell the drivers which way to go. **Topic sentences** direct readers, they tell them what the subject of a paragraph is. Careful writers put topic sentences in their paragraphs to keep a reader traveling on the right road.

A topic sentence states briefly an idea that is more fully developed in a paragraph. A topic sentence can appear anywhere in a paragraph. It can be at the beginning of a paragraph or at the end, or at both the beginning and the end. It can also be in the middle of a paragraph. Or a topic sentence can be implied, or suggested — not written out at all.

Here are examples of topic sentences used in five different ways:

TOPIC SENTENCE AT THE BEGINNING

Americans make no distinction in greeting friends, acquaintances, elders, or superiors. When Americans see close friends, casual acquaintances, teachers, or even someone they know only by sight, they are likely to say "Hi" in all cases. This does not mean that they have no more regard for friends than for casual acquaintances. It only means that "Hi" serves as a greeting for both.

A topic sentence often appears as the first sentence in an English paragraph. This paragraph pattern is popular because it is easier for both a reader and a writer. A writer who first announces his or her topic and then goes on to develop the topic tells a reader from the start where the paragraph is leading. If a topic sentence is placed at the beginning of a paragraph, a writer can more quickly glance up at it as he or she completes his paragraph. Doing this constantly reminds a writer what the topic is. Checking the topic sentence as you write helps to prevent random ideas from entering your paragraph.

Beginning a paragraph with a topic sentence is the most useful way for a student to start practicing writing English paragraphs.

TOPIC SENTENCE AT THE BEGINNING AND END

Good manners are important in all countries, but ways of expressing good manners are different from country to country. Americans eat with knives and forks; Japanese eat with chopsticks. Americans say "Hi" when they meet; Japanese bow. Many American men open doors for women; Japanese men do not. On the surface, it appears that good manners in America are not good manners in Japan, and in a way this is true. But in any country, the only manners that are important are those involving one person's behavior toward another person. In all countries it is good manners to behave considerately toward others and bad manners not to. *It is only the way of behaving politely that differs from country to country.*

Sometimes a writer will want to give really strong emphasis to a topic sentence. When this happens, a writer can place a topic sentence at both the beginning and end of a paragraph. This can tell a reader that the idea in this paragraph is more important than other ideas found in other paragraphs.

The example paragraph begins with a topic sentence and ends with a restatement of the same topic sentence. Here the important idea that "ways of expressing good manners are different from country to country" opens the paragraph. Then the writer sums up the paragraph in the last sentence. The reader is reminded in these new words of the paragraph's main point: "the way of behaving politely . . . differs from country to country."

TOPIC SENTENCE IN THE MIDDLE

Californians and New Englanders are both American. They speak the same language and abide by the same federal laws. *But they are very different in their ways of life.* Mobility — both physical and psychological — has made a great impression on the culture of Californians; lack of mobility is the mark of the customs and morality of New Englanders.

The example paragraph shows a good reason for placing a topic sentence in the middle of a paragraph. This is a helpful approach when you are writing about how things are alike (comparison) or how they are different (contrast). Notice that the example paragraph opens with two sentences that point out how Californians and New Englanders are *similar*. Then the topic sentence acts as a transition to two closing sentences that discuss how Californians and New Englanders are *different* from each other.

The writer has arranged the paragraph in two ways so that the differences, not the similarities, are the main point. First, because the writer starts to discuss similarities, the transition topic sentence must focus on differences. If the writer had organized the other way around — beginning with differences — the transition topic sentence would stress similarities. Second, by ending with a discussion of differences, the writer places this information in the most forceful part of the paragraph.

TOPIC SENTENCE AT THE END

Americans might be embarrassed because their Japanese friends are so formal with them. Japanese might feel insulted because American acquaintances greet them casually. Still, the forms of greeting in both countries only show respect for others. *It just happens that Americans and Japanese have a different way of looking at human relationships and thus have a different way of showing respect.*

Placing a topic sentence at the end of a paragraph results in a dramatic paragraph. By not stating a topic sentence until the last sentence, a writer creates a feeling of suspense that makes a reader want to keep on reading. A trained writer knows that the last sentence of a paragraph is the sentence that will probably be best remembered by a reader. This is true for two reasons: (1) A reader often only skims through the body of a paragraph. But a reader's attention focuses on the final sentence because it often sums up a writer's central point; (2) Since a reader absorbs a final sentence last, the idea of the final sentence is more likely to make a lasting impression on the reader than ideas read earlier in a paragraph.

TOPIC SENTENCE IMPLIED

First you must wait for a sunny day. Remember that the rays of the sun are most direct between 11 A.M. and 2 P.M. This is the time when you will tan the quickest. At the right time and on the right day, pick an open spot outdoors and lay out a large towel or beach mat. You may want to bring along several things: suntan oil, a portable radio, a book or magazine, sunglasses, a pillow. It is a good idea not to stay in the sun too long at first. Begin with a half hour, and then gradually increase the time you spend in the sun. Certain parts of your body will burn more quickly than others. These include the backs of your knees, the insides of your elbows, your shoulders, and your nose. Be sure to cover these spots with suntan oil when you first go outside. Cover them again with oil after you have been out in the sun for a while.

(Possible implied topic sentence: Taking a sunbath calls for careful planning.)

Paragraphs, such as the preceding one, can be written that do not have topic sentences expressed. Such topic sentences are called "implied." But this kind of treatment of a topic sentence is best saved until a writer has control over the four ways of stating a topic sentence.

A paragraph that has an implied topic sentence can be an interesting contrast to other paragraphs that have topic sentences expressed. Yet a writer needs to be careful in shaping paragraphs with implied topic sentences. The chances are greater that a reader will miss the point if a topic sentence is implied. And, if a topic sentence is implied, a writer may more easily lose track of the topic being developed.

TEST YOURSELF

In this paragraph, the topic sentence is missing. Read the paragraph closely. Then answer the questions below it.

At several long counters, students can quickly receive their lunches. Tables and chairs are plentiful and well spaced. The lighting is bright. Walls are painted a cheerful color. A large number of trash baskets placed around the room make cleanup easy.

1. The main topic of all the sentences in the paragraph is _____.
2. The point that the writer is making about the cafeteria is that it is: (Write out the correct letter and word.)

   A. Unpleasant   B. Good   C. Poor

   _____

3. Write a topic sentence for this paragraph that both states the topic and gives an opinion about it. _____

   _____

   _____

   _____

Find answers to TEST YOURSELF on page 120.

FOURTEEN WAYS TO POLISH YOUR SKILLS

Activity 15

Copy these paragraphs on the lines below. Then underline the topic sentences. If a topic sentence does not appear but is implied, add one.

1. Eating lunch is one of my favorite pastimes. Because lunch comes in the middle of the day, it gives me a welcome break from studying. At school, lunch means thirty minutes out of class and a chance to rest

after the morning's work. While eating, I can plan what I'm going to do in the afternoon. And besides offering a pleasant break in the day, lunch is always a good meal.

_____

_____

_____

_____

_____

_____

_____

_____

_____

_____

2. Baby-sitting with my little brother is no fun. Just as I settle down to read or watch television, he demands that I play with him. If I get a telephone call, he screams in the background or knocks something over. I always have to hang up to find out what's wrong with him. He refuses to let me eat a snack in peace. Usually he wants half of whatever I have to eat. Then, when he finally grows tired, it takes about an hour for him to fall asleep.

---

3. A bus driver must answer questions while guiding a bus through heavy traffic. All day long the driver answers the same questions without becoming angry. Every few minutes a bus driver has to ask passengers to step to the rear of the bus. In spite of traffic snarls and thoughtless passengers who cause delays, a bus driver is expected to cover his or her route on schedule.

---

4. It is often said that lightning never strikes twice in the same place. But this is not true. Go ask the forest rangers. Rangers who spend their summers as fire fighters will tell you that every thunderstorm brings several bolts of lightning to their craggy lookout stations. Not only can lightning strike twice in the same place, it is likely to. The familiar saying actually states the opposite of what really happens during an electrical storm.

_____

_____

_____

_____

_____

_____

_____

_____

_____

_____

_____

5. People who live in cities today think that meat is something that comes wrapped in cellophane from the supermarket, potatoes come by the pound in plastic or paper bags, and feathers grow in hats. The city dwellers' views are quite different from the views of their ancestors, who knew that meat is hunted down in the forest, potatoes are planted and weeded, and only birds can produce feathers. Yet, whether people today realize it or not, they are still as dependent on animals and plants for their existence as their ancestors were.

_____

_____

_____

_____

_____

_____

_____

_____

_____

_____

_____

_____

_____

_____

_____

_____

_____

6. If an insect were to irritate a hair of the Venus's fly-trap just once, no change would take place. But if within sixty seconds another shock were applied, the leaves of the plant would quickly snap shut. For here we have a remarkable example of a plant that needs more than one shock to cause the tightening of the leaves.

_____

_____

_____

_____

_____

_____

_____

_____

_____

_____

_____

7. English is full of words that have gradually changed their meanings. One example is the word *graft*. The verb *to graft* first meant merely "to work." English people once used the word in such expressions as "Where are you grafting?," meaning "Where are you working?" From this perfectly respectable meaning, the word has gradually changed. Today *graft* refers to illegal gains won by dishonest politicians.

_____

_____

_____

_____

_____

_____

_____

_____

_____

_____

_____

_____

_____

8. Electronic microscopes reveal the physical appearance of objects that are many times smaller than ever before seen. Huge radio telescopes explore areas of the sky previously not known to human vision. The scientific wonders of this age we live in continue to grow. Computers store reams of facts in information banks. Atomic-powered submarines prowl the oceans without refueling. Man-made satellites hurtle through space at incredible speeds.

_____

_____

_____

_____

_____

_____

_____

_____

_____

_____

_____

_____

9. Human blood serves the body in three important ways. First, blood carries substances needed to maintain and repair the body tissues. In this way, blood serves as a provider. Second, blood also serves as a disposer, since it carries wastes and gases away from the tissues of the body. In addition, blood acts as a defender. The white corpuscles in the bloodstream constantly guard against and try to destroy bacteria and other agents that threaten the body's welfare.

_____

_____

_____

_____

_____

_____

_____

_____

_____

_____

_____

_____

_____

10. Because I wanted to photograph a scorpion but did not have my close-up lens, I asked Ramon if he would catch a scorpion for me. He managed to find a large scorpion with twenty babies on its back. We

put the scorpion in a jar for my return to town. Marta explained that she had been stung twice before. She said that the sting is always very painful. If the venom in the scorpion is strong, the victim's mouth becomes anesthetized, as it does when a dentist injects novocaine. And the scorpion's sting could be fatal. The woman's fear of scorpions made me glad that Ramon, a man who knew how to give injections of serum, was with us.

_____

_____

_____

_____

_____

_____

_____

_____

_____

_____

_____

_____

_____

_____

_____

_____

Activity 16

Unscramble these ten groups of sentences by first choosing one as the topic sentence. List its number on line A. Write the remaining sentence numbers in correct order on the remaining lines. Then write out the correct paragraph on the lines that follow.

1) A._____ (Topic Sentence)

   B._____

   C._____

   D._____

  1. And the hogans (Navaho dwellings) are still standing, though some of them now have red roofs.

  2. Nor have their customs changed very much, even if their tribal councils meet in handsome ranch houses owned by the tribe.

  3. Actually, Navaho life is in very little danger of disappearing.

  4. True, there were far more pickup trucks than wagons on the Navaho reservation, but many families still have wagons, and most own horses.

_____

_____

_____

_____

_____

_____

_____

_____

_____

_____

_____

_____

_____

_____

_____

_____

_____

2) A._____ (Topic Sentence)

   B._____

   C._____

   D._____
   1. These domestic presentations are usually made in December.
   2. Foreign cars and trucks are usually displayed later.
   3. Then you can see the new developments in the Ford, General Motors, and American Motor car lines.
   4. Automobile manufacturers have been planning for months to present their new models to the public.

_____

_____

_____

_____

_____

_____

_____

_____

_____

_____

_____

_____

_____

3) A._____ (Topic Sentence)

   B._____

   C._____

   D._____

1. In addition, the state has magnificent scenery and superb highways.
2. Californians, who think nothing of driving over four hundred miles from San Francisco to Los Angeles for a weekend visit, or to Mexico for a short vacation, have several reasons for their mobility.
3. But perhaps the most important reason for their mobility is that most Californians have a pioneering tradition.
4. First, despite a rapidly increasing population, California still offers a lot of room to move around in.

_____

_____

_____

_____

_____

_____

_____

_____

_____

_____

_____

_____

_____

_____

_____

_____

_____

_____

_____

4) A._____ (Topic Sentence)

   B._____

C._____

D._____

1. However, one thing some of them never seem to get used to is American food.
2. When people from Asian countries come to the United States, it takes them quite a while to get used to American ways.
3. Over a period of time, though, these newcomers do become accustomed to American ways.
4. They find much in America that seems strange to them; indeed, *everything* seems strange at first.

_____

_____

_____

_____

_____

_____

_____

_____

_____

_____

_____

_____

5) A._____ (Topic Sentence)

B._____

C._____

D._____

1. The Grand Canyon may be a wonderful sight, as it was for the Spaniards, or a scientific event, or a religious experience — and it may well be all three.

2. The first white men looked into the great canyon in 1540.
3. The greatest sight of all, unparalleled in the world, and one that everyone wants to see is the Grand Canyon.
4. They were a side party scouting from Coronado's main force, and they were awestruck.

_____

_____

_____

_____

_____

_____

_____

_____

_____

_____

_____

_____

6) A._____ (Topic Sentence)

   B._____

   C._____

   D._____

   E._____

1. For example, you don't need many clothes.
2. However, despite these advantages, those who have lived in warm climates and in cold climates often prefer a cold climate because it is less monotonous and offers winter sports.
3. In addition, you don't have to shovel snow or pay heating bills.

4. Living in a place where the weather is always warm has its advantages.
5. You can wear lightweight, inexpensive, and easy-to-clean cotton clothing all year.

_____

_____

_____

_____

_____

_____

_____

_____

_____

_____

_____

_____

7) A._____ (Topic Sentence)

   B._____

   C._____

   D._____

   E._____

1. They never seem to be working.
2. It seems to workers that students lead easy lives only because students work and relax at different times from workers.
3. Working people sometimes think that college students live a very easy life.
4. The truth is, though, that most students spend as many hours in class or at their studies as workers do at their jobs.

5. To them it appears that students have little to do: they sleep late, talk for hours over coffee, and go to parties every night.

_____

_____

_____

_____

_____

_____

_____

_____

_____

_____

_____

_____

_____

_____

_____

8) A._____ (Topic Sentence)

   B._____

   C._____

   D._____

   E._____

1. Now that color television has been improved, it is enjoyed by many families in the United States.
2. Almost every home, no matter how poor, has a television set.
3. Television is popular not because it offers excellent entertainment but because it allows viewers to escape from life's problems.

4. Many homes have two or more TV sets — perhaps a portable television for the teenagers in the family and a large set for the parents.
5. Television is big business in the United States.

_____

_____

_____

_____

_____

_____

_____

_____

_____

_____

_____

_____

_____

_____

_____

_____

9) A._____ (Topic Sentence)

   B._____

   C._____

   D._____

   E._____

1. For another, the hairs on a glove, when placed under a microscope, may provide important information.

2. A single glove at the scene of a crime may provide valuable clues for the police.

3. If not, they may give away the criminal's own hair color or perhaps the fact that he has been where there are farm animals.

4. For one thing, the size and style of a glove may suggest the build of the criminal and his way of life — one glove may direct the search toward a large man used to driving a truck; another glove may suggest a small, dapper, "society" man.

5. If the hairs match those of the victim, they may link the owner to the crime.

_____

_____

_____

_____

_____

_____

_____

_____

_____

_____

_____

_____

_____

_____

_____

_____

_____

_____

_____

_____

_____

_____

_____

10) A._____ (Topic Sentence)

    B._____

    C._____

    D._____

    E._____

1. Another shallow reason is the young man's desire to meet a rich woman among the motion-picture stars and other celebrities who fly the airways.
2. Wearing the uniform is a sign for all to see that he has passed the tests of efficiency, pose, and general fitness.
3. Surveys show that not all of the reasons for becoming an airline steward are based on sound thinking.
4. Finally, there is the lure of competition.
5. One of the superficial reasons is the advice offered by relatives, teachers, and friends; a second is the belief that the life of an airline steward is filled with adventure and excitement.

_____

_____

_____

_____

_____

_____

_____

_____

_____

_____

_____

_____
_____
_____
_____
_____
_____
_____
_____
_____

Activity 17

*Revise paragraph 1 in Activity 15 so that it **ends** with a topic sentence.*

_____
_____
_____
_____
_____
_____
_____
_____
_____
_____

Activity 18

*Revise paragraph 3 in Activity 15 so that it **begins** with a topic sentence.*

_____
_____

_____

_____

_____

_____

_____

_____

_____

_____

_____

_____

_____

_____

Activity 19

Revise paragraph 7 in Activity 15 so that it both **begins and ends** _with a topic sentence._

_____

_____

_____

_____

_____

_____

_____

_____

_____

_____

_____

_____

_____

_____

Activity 20

Revise paragraph 2 in Activity 15 so that its topic sentence **falls within** *the paragraph.*

_____

_____

_____

_____

_____

_____

_____

_____

_____

_____

_____

_____

_____

_____

_____

Activity 21

Revise paragraph 9 in Activity 15 so that its topic sentence is **implied or suggested.**

_____

_____

_____

_____

_____

_____

_____

_____

_____

_____

_____

_____

_____

_____

Activity 22

Write a short paragraph (at least four sentences) that **begins** *with either of these topic sentences:*

1. When it is time to eat, many people satisfy their hunger in fast-food restaurants.
2. Hairstyling can be done in a shop by a hairstylist, or you can learn to do it yourself at home.

_____

_____

_____

_____

_____

_____

_____

_____
_____
_____
_____
_____
_____
_____
_____
_____

Activity 23

*Write a short paragraph that **ends** with either of these two topic sentences:*

1. These examples show how popular amusement parks have become.
2. In any of these locations, camping can be one of the most delightful activities.

_____
_____
_____
_____
_____
_____
_____
_____
_____
_____
_____
_____
_____

_____

_____

_____

_____

Activity 24

Write a short paragraph that both **begins and ends** _with either pair of topic sentences._

BEGINNING OF PARAGRAPH	Many popular television shows use violence to improve their ratings.
END OF PARAGRAPH	Only the future can tell whether the popularity of violence on television will be a lasting trend.
BEGINNING OF PARAGRAPH	All of the ways of playing music — records, cassette tapes, cartridges, and reel-to-reel tapes — have both advantages and disadvantages.
END OF PARAGRAPH	A listener has to weigh the advantages and disadvantages of these four sources of sound, selecting the one that seems best.

_____

_____

_____

_____

_____

_____

_____

_____

_____

_____

_____

_____

_____

_____

_____

_____

_____

_____

_____

_____

_____

_____

_____

Activity 25

*Write a short paragraph that has either of these topic sentences **within** the paragraph.*

1. These are the decisions you have to weigh when choosing a college to attend.
2. These are the paperbacks I am most interested in reading.

_____

_____

_____

_____

_____

_____

_____

_____

_____

_____

_____

_____

_____

_____

_____

_____

Activity 26

Write a short paragraph that has either of these two sentences as its **implied** *topic sentence.*

1. There are a number of different ways to do homework.
2. There are a number of different ways to diet.

_____

_____

_____

_____

_____

_____

_____

_____

_____

_____

_____

_____

_____

_____

_____

Activity 27

Write a short, original paragraph **beginning** *with a topic sentence.*

_____

_____

_____

_____

_____

_____

_____

_____

_____

_____

_____

_____

_____

_____

_____

_____

_____

_____

_____

_____

_____

_____

Activity 28

Write a short, original paragraph **ending** _with a topic sentence._

_____

_____

_____

_____

_____

_____

_____

_____

_____

_____

_____

_____

_____

_____

_____

_____

_____

_____

_____

_____

_____

_____

ANSWERS to TEST YOURSELF   1. the cafeteria (or lunchroom)
2. B. Good
3. Our cafeteria is a pleasant place to eat lunch.

TOPIC SENTENCE POST-TEST

1. Write out the paragraph's topic sentence on the lines below the paragraph.

Lumber is still an important business in the United States in spite of the growing popularity of synthetic building materials. Much of the lumbering industry is based in the Pacific Northwest. Lumber comes from two great classes of trees: the softwoods (or conifers) and the hardwoods (or dicotyledons). The softwoods include the familiar and useful evergreens, such as pine, fir, cypress, some cedar, and the giant California redwood. From the hardwoods comes an even greater variety: ash, beech, hickory, elm, maple, walnut, sycamore, eucalyptus, teak, and various kinds of mahogany. All these hardwoods supply huge quantities of valuable wood each year.

_____

_____

_____

_____

_____

2. Look at the cartoons at the beginning of Chapters 1, 2, 3, and 7. Use the idea in each cartoon as the basis for writing a topic sentence. Write out the four topic sentences on the lines below.

Chapter 1: _____

_____

_____

Chapter 2: _____

_____

_____

Chapter 3: _____

_____

_____

Chapter 7: _____

_____

_____

_____

5 CONTROLLING IDEA

A backpack that is well filled keeps you alive in the wilderness. And a topic sentence that includes a controlling idea keeps a writer's purpose alive in a paragraph.

CONTROLLING IDEA PRE-TEST

1. Write out the words that express the controlling ideas in these topic sentences. (A controlling idea tells how a paragraph will be developed.)

EXAMPLE: You follow eight steps in changing an automobile tire.

    eight steps

1. Most successful movies have a few qualities in common.

2. A person can look for a job in several different ways.

3. Homeowners can order various kinds of telephone service.

    _____

4. There are many advantages and disadvantages to the fast-food restaurant chains in the United States.

    _____

5. People pick up materials to read for many reasons.

    _____

2. List the controlling idea in the topic sentence of the paragraph found in question 1, p. 121. Then write out the controlling ideas in the three sentences you wrote based on the cartoons opening Chapters 4–6, p. 88.

    1. _____

    Chapter 4: _____

    Chapter 5: _____

    Chapter 6: _____

A **controlling idea** is a word or group of words that gives the main thought of a paragraph. These important words make up part or all of a topic sentence. A controlling idea helps both a reader and a writer. It helps a reader by telling what a paragraph's main subject will be. A controlling idea helps a writer by reminding him or her at all times to keep to the central idea as he or she writes a paragraph.

In the following three topic sentences, the sentences on the left do not contain strong controlling ideas. Specific controlling ideas have been added to these three topic sentences on the right (the controlling ideas are boldfaced):

Too General	*Specific Controlling Idea Added*
1. Students often ride to school.	Some students drive **cars** to school and others ride **bicycles, mopeds,** or **motorcycles.** (This paragraph will be developed in four parts: (1) information about cars; (2) information about bicycles; (3) information about mopeds; (4) information about motorcycles.)
2. My brother enjoys water sports.	Among the water sports that my brother enjoys most are **snorkeling, scuba diving,** and **waterskiing.**

(This paragraph will be developed in three parts: (1) information about snorkeling; (2) information about scuba diving; (3) information about waterskiing.)

3. *Star Wars* and *Close Encounters of a Third Kind* are interesting movies.

Star Wars and *Close Encounters of a Third Kind* are very **different** kinds of science fiction movies.

(This paragraph will be developed by discussing the *differences* between the two films. Points might include which film is more humorous, which is more imaginative, which is more fantastic, or which has the most advanced special effects.)

Choosing a specific controlling idea before you write a paragraph takes time. And making sure that the controlling idea you have chosen is the *best* one to introduce what you want to say in a paragraph takes still more time. But doing this saves you a great deal of work once you begin to write. Often, a well-chosen controlling idea will suggest an outline that you can follow in writing a paragraph.

You can see from the three examples given that it would be much simpler to write a paragraph by using the specific controlling ideas on the right than by using the general ones on the left.

Sometimes most of a sentence is needed to express a controlling idea:

We spent **a day at the beach.**

Sometimes only a word or two is needed to express a controlling idea:

There are **five rules** to follow in leading a dog through obedience training.

When you are developing a controlling idea to place in a topic sentence, keep these guidelines in mind:

1. Make your controlling idea as *specific* as possible. (Note that sometimes a more general statement also works well. The third example given earlier is more general than the first two.) Writing from a controlling idea will help prevent you from adding unrelated facts and ideas to your paragraph. You can continually check back to the controlling idea to keep yourself on the right track.

2. Make sure that the controlling idea you choose really states the subject you want to develop. For example, if you wanted to write a paragraph about the most frightening scenes in Walt Disney movies, it would be a mistake to write a topic sentence with this controlling idea:

In Walt Disney movies, cartoon art reached **new heights of excellence.** (Controlling idea boldfaced)

A much better topic sentence/controlling idea would be this:

Every Walt Disney movie has its share of **frightening scenes.** (Controlling idea boldfaced)

3. Make sure that your controlling idea will break down into the right number of parts to be written about in a paragraph. Sometimes a paragraph will deal with only one aspect of a subject. In these cases, a controlling idea like this would be appropriate:

Television commercials are often very **imaginative.**

A paragraph written from this controlling idea would contain examples of imaginative television commercials.

Many other times, though, a more specific controlling idea will suggest the parts that can be written about in a paragraph. For example, your topic sentence/controlling idea might be this:

Many people enjoy **aerial sports.**

The controlling idea *aerial sports* is a good one because it suggests several different parts — piloting an airplane, gliding, hang gliding, free falling, and parachuting — that could be developed in a paragraph.

Study these four paragraphs that are developed from controlling ideas (boldfaced) placed in beginning topic sentences:

1. You can patch a bicycle tire in **several simple steps.** First you have to find the spot where the leak is. Then scrape the leaky place so the glue will stick when you patch the hole. Next, put glue on the tire patch. While the glue is drying, check to make sure that the area around the leak is rough enough to hold the patch. Now put the patch on the tire. Let the patch dry before you try to pump up the tire again.

Notice that all six sentences that follow the opening topic sentence explain the controlling idea of *several simple steps.* The steps are listed in the order that they would happen.

2. Yesterday at the swimming pool everything seemed to go wrong. Soon after I arrived, I sat on my sunglasses and broke them. Later my bathing suit caught on the rough edge of a chair, tearing a hole in the side of the suit. But my worst moment came when I decided to climb up to the high diving tower to see what the view was like. Once I was up there, I

realized that my friends were looking at me because they thought I was going to dive. I decided I was too afraid to dive from that height. So I climbed down the ladder, feeling very embarrassed.

In this paragraph, the writer develops the controlling idea of *everything seeming to go wrong* by discussing three incidents — the broken sunglasses, the torn bathing suit, and climbing down from the high diving tower. The writer knows when to end the paragraph and stops writing because there are no more things that went wrong to discuss.

3. **A teaspoon** is a utensil for scooping up and carrying small amounts of something. It has two parts: a flat, narrow tapered handle, by which it is held, and a shallow oval bowl to dip and carry liquid, food, or other materials. The handle is about four inches long. It arches slightly upward at the wide end, and it curves sharply downward at the narrow end. The shape of the handle allows it to fit easily in the hand. It is correctly held resting across the third finger and grasped between the thumb and first joint of the forefinger of the right hand. When the bowl is level, the handle points upward at a shallow angle. A spoon is usually made of metal or some other hard-wearing, unbreakable material.

Since this paragraph defines and describes a teaspoon, every sentence in the paragraph should give information about a teaspoon. The eight sentences do this. Each one expands on the controlling idea of *teaspoon* found in the opening topic sentence.

4. There was a **serious accident** in the chemistry lab last week. A confused student accidentally poured a wrong mixture of chemicals in a test tube. There was a strong explosion. Broken pieces of glass from the test tube flew in all directions. A sliver of flying glass found its mark in John Martin's right arm. The lab instructor saw blood trickling from John's arm. He immediately notified the university's infirmary about the accident.

The writer here uses the controlling idea of *serious accident* to guide the paragraph development. Each sentence relates to the sentence coming before it and leads into the sentence following it. All six sentences focus *only* on the controlling idea of the accident in the chemistry lab.

TEST YOURSELF

Read the following paragraph. Then answer the questions below it.

Helen is the most conceited person I know. She thinks she knows everything and can do anything. According to her, she is an expert bowler, tennis player, swimmer, and softball player. She tells everyone she meets that she is the smartest person in her class. No matter what the problem is, Helen is sure she can solve it because she believes there is nothing she cannot do.

1. What is the author's topic? (Write the correct letter and word on the line below.)

   A. Conceit   B. The importance of sports   C. Helen

   _____

2. Write out the paragraph's topic sentence. _____

   _____

   _____

3. What word or words tell the topic sentence's controlling idea? _____

   _____

Find answers to TEST YOURSELF on page 136.

SIX WAYS TO POLISH YOUR SKILLS

Activity 29

Write out the controlling ideas in these topic sentences.

1. Many different kinds of part-time jobs are available.

   _____

2. People try many ways to improve their looks.

   _____

3. Students have various reasons for choosing where they want to sit in a classroom.

   _____

4. Some holidays are more festive than others.

   _____

5. Developing a plan for organizing a locker is important.

   _____

6. Society is trying many different approaches to discourage people from smoking.

   _____

7. A young person needs to learn how to become self-reliant.

_____

8. Parents have different ways of giving their children an education.

_____

9. Studying for tests calls for a methodical approach.

_____

10. Certain guidelines help a family to live together happily.

_____

Activity 30

Revise the following topic sentence by adding controlling ideas when necessary. Circle all controlling ideas.

EXAMPLE: (No control-   Las Vegas is a city with gambling casinos.
            ling idea)

            (Improved   Las Vegas offers (many ways to gamble.)
            by adding
            controlling
            idea)

1. My families own pets.

_____

_____

2. I like television horror movies.

_____

_____

3. People develop their own life-styles.

_____

_____

4. Some people like to take baths.

_____

_____

5. Comic books are entertaining.

_____

6. Blue jeans are popular.

_____

_____

7. Magazines are interesting.

_____

_____

8. Poise is important.

_____

_____

9. Surfing is a water sport.

_____

_____

10. A person needs to have a healthy self-image.

_____

_____

Activity 31

Step 1: *Develop the following words into specific controlling ideas.*
Step 2: *Expand the controlling ideas into topic sentences.*

EXAMPLE: **weather**

Step 1:   lightning, thunder, and hail

Step 2:   Yesterday the biggest storm of the year
                           brought us thunder, lightning, and hail.

1. **movie**
   Step 1: _____

_____

Step 2: _____
_____
_____
_____
_____

2. trip
   Step 1: _____
_____

   Step 2: _____
_____
_____
_____
_____

3. situation
   Step 1: _____
_____

   Step 2: _____
_____
_____
_____
_____

4. musical instruments
   Step 1: _____
_____

   Step 2: _____
_____

_____

_____

_____

_____

5. moods

   Step 1: _____

_____

   Step 2: _____

_____

_____

_____

_____

6. experience

   Step 1: _____

_____

   Step 2: _____

_____

_____

_____

7. game

   Step 1: _____

_____

   Step 2: _____

_____

_____

_____

_____

8. decision

Step 1: _____

_____

Step 2: _____

_____

_____

_____

9. teachers

Step 1: _____

_____

Step 2: _____

_____

_____

_____

10. achievements

Steps 1: _____

_____

Step 2: _____

_____

_____

_____

Activity 32

Write a short paragraph beginning with either of these two topic sentences. Develop your paragraph from the controlling idea.

1. Everyone has favorite foods, and I am no exception.
2. When I feel bored, I find ways to entertain myself.

_____
_____
_____
_____
_____
_____
_____
_____
_____
_____
_____
_____
_____
_____
_____
_____
_____
_____
_____
_____
_____
_____

Activity 33

Do another revision of the three revised controlling ideas on pp. 124–125. Base your revision on information about transportation, sports, or movies with which you are familiar. Then write a short paragraph developed from one revised topic sentence and controlling idea.

_____

_____

_____

_____

_____

_____

_____

_____

_____

_____

_____

_____

_____

_____

_____

_____

_____

_____

_____

_____

Activity 34

Write a paragraph on any subject. Begin the paragraph with a topic sentence that has a controlling idea. Make every sentence in your paragraph relate to its controlling idea.

_____

_____

_____

_____
_____
_____
_____
_____
_____
_____
_____
_____
_____
_____
_____
_____
_____
_____
_____
_____
_____
_____
_____
_____
_____

ANSWERS to TEST YOURSELF
1. A. Conceit
2. Helen is the most conceited person I know.
3. Conceited

CONTROLLING IDEA POST-TEST

1) Write out the words that express the controlling ideas in these sentences.

EXAMPLE: I like three kinds of pizza.

           three kinds

1. Julian wrote a number of suggestions to the student newspaper about low-cost housing.

   _____

2. Some of these time-honored customs seem "old-fashioned" to many people.

   _____

3. The Sierra Club, the Cousteau Society, and the Audubon Society are environmental organizations that provide many valuable services.

   _____

4. The marriage counselor mentioned two strategies for avoiding arguments before breakfast.

   _____

5. It is surprising that there are so few women working in professions because there are many benefits in these jobs.

   _____

2) List the controlling idea in the topic sentence of the paragraph found in question 1, p. 87. Then write out the controlling ideas in the four sentences you wrote based on the cartoons opening Chapters 1, 2, 3, and 7, p. 121.

     1. _____

   Chapter 1: _____

   Chapter 2: _____

   Chapter 3: _____

   Chapter 4: _____

6 UNITY

A violinist's music does not fit with a rock band's beat. Removing the violinist produces a unified sound. A writer gains unity in the same way by cutting out any thoughts that do not fit in with a paragraph's controlling idea.

UNITY PRE-TEST

Find the sentence that does not fit logically into the paragraph. Then write it out on the lines below.

Foreign students at an American university often get a wrong idea of what people in the United States are like. Because visiting students don't often meet a housewife, a laborer, an office worker, or an average commuter, foreign students only get to know other students really well. From seeing the work habits of North American students, foreign students get the impression that all North Americans are always very busy. After all, these native students seem always to be on the move, never relaxing. One good way to relax is to practice yoga. But foreign students don't realize that North American students are among the busiest people in the United States. Taking four or five courses a semester gives them a work load that is sometimes staggering. Most teachers give two or three examinations during a term, and many assign daily readings or written assignments, as well as term papers. Because of this, students at United States universities have to continue studying throughout a semester. They cannot wait until the end of the semester and then cram for finals — something many European university students succeed in doing.

_____

_____

_____

A well-written paragraph must have **unity.** That is, each paragraph is a block or unit of thought. It should present only one topic or one part of a topic. A paragraph states a single thought. All the facts, examples, and reasons in a unified paragraph should explain this thought. All material not properly related to the rest of the paragraph should be left out.

Unity helps a writer speak clearly to a reader. A writer builds a paragraph by making every sentence refer to the controlling idea found in the topic sentence. Unity is important in any type of writing — business letter, essay question, or term report.

Look at this example of a unified paragraph:

(1) In rock music there is a distinct and almost overwhelming beat. (2) No single beat is characteristic of the music today. (3) But each song has an easily recognizable rhythm. (4) As you listen to a song, your foot usually starts to pick up the beat. (5) Before long, your entire body seems to be moving with it. (6) Your head pounds with the beat, and there is no room for thought. (7) Only the surge of the music is important. (8) In its own way, rock music is as dominant as the Rock of Gibraltar. (9) Its message is an overpowering emotional one.

First, let us pick out the topic sentence in this paragraph. Do you agree that it is the first one: "In rock music there is a distinct and almost overwhelming beat."? The word "beat" gives us the controlling idea of this paragraph. Notice how well the writer ties every sentence to the idea of the _beat_ of rock music.

The writer does this chiefly by word repetition. The word "beat" is repeated in sentences 2, 4, and 6. "Rhythm," another way of saying "beat," appears in sentence 3. "Surge," also a synonym, is in sentence 7. The pronoun "it" in sentence 5 refers back to "beat." And in the last two sentences, the writer restates and sums up the opening statement about rock music. From the first sentence to the last, this is a tightly unified paragraph. It contains no information that is not related to rock music and its beat.

Here is a second paragraph to examine for unity:

(1) This drive to compete and to be a "winner" has always been part of the American psyche. (2) Our early ancestors were aggressive and competitive. (3) They knew they were pitted against amazing odds, but they also felt they were a select and chosen group. (4) They defied their mother country and were successful. (5) Later came the "frontier spirit," the belief in survival of the fittest, and the growing American fetish for figures, statistics, records, and winners. (6) Over forty years ago, John R. Tunis wrote, in *The American Way in Sport:* "We worship the victors. (7) But why? (8) The Dutch don't especially, nor the Swedes, neither do the Danes, the Swiss, or the English, and they all seem fairly civilized people." (9) We devised an international "scoreboard" to chart our successes in the Olympics as well as in our wars, an obsession that was tragically reflected in our approach to Vietnam, where President Johnson and President Nixon vowed that each was not going down in history as "the first American President who lost a war."

Here the topic sentence is again the first one. The words "this drive . . . to be a winner" express the paragraph's controlling idea. Notice that, in maintaining unity, the author dips into history to use a time development. The writer talks first about aggressive early ancestors, and then moves forward in time to mention the competitive frontier spirit.

Still moving forward, the writer quotes from an American book of forty years ago about worshiping the victors, and then his central idea is summarized by comparing the American need to win in athletics with the need of two American presidents to win in warfare.

The paragraph opens with the subject of winning. It ends by discussing the opposite of winning: losing. But throughout the paragraph, the focus is the same. No sentence contains information that is not central to the main idea stated in the opening sentence. Like the first example paragraph, this one is unified.

Third, examine this paragraph for unity:

(1) The saying "One picture is worth 1,000 words" suggests the importance to a writer of thinking by examples. (2) By putting the right examples in a paragraph or composition, a writer can tell his or her idea to a reader. (3) But the art of using the right examples is not easy to learn. (4) *Choosing* examples calls for imagination. (5) *Using* examples well calls for both reasoning and control. (6) Ex-

amples must make abstract ideas more concrete. (7) At the same time, examples must not lead a reader away from a writer's central purpose. (8) Clear thinking is needed for good writing. (9) Clear thinking alone helps a writer choose examples that will explain the idea of an essay. (10) You must have a plan instead of a grocery list. (11) You must write with your mind as well as your pen because a composition is an act of thought.

Once again, the opening topic sentence contains the controlling idea of the paragraph: thinking by examples. This is really a two-part idea. It deals with both thinking and examples. Realizing this, the writer speaks about examples for the first half of the paragraph. Note that the word "examples" is repeated to maintain unity in sentences 2 through 7.

Then, in the second half of the paragraph, the writer shifts to discuss how examples relate to thinking. The word "thinking" appears in sentences 8 and 9; the related words "plan" and "mind" appear in sentences 10 and 11, respectively.

Like the writer of the first example paragraph, this writer has insured unity for a paragraph by careful word repetition. But both writers have avoided the danger of *monotonous* word repetition by using varied methods of stressing the central idea in each sentence. These other devices include a pronoun *(it)*, a synonym (a word that means the same thing as another word), and a word or phrase that means *nearly* the same thing as the controlling idea.

TEST YOURSELF

1. *Choose four sentences from the list below to fit in the correct order into the paragraph beginning with the topic sentence "Kathy is athletic."*

   a. Sue is intelligent.
   b. She is an excellent fencer.
   c. She has won many swimming awards.
   d. The girls in my class are quite different from each other.
   e. Linda is an artist.
   f. Her teammates chose her to be captain of the basketball team.
   g. Carol is the best dancer in school.
   h. No one in school can catch up with her at the track meets.

   TS: Kathy is athletic.

   1._____

   2._____

3._____

4._____

2. *Choose one of the sentences from the a.-h. list as the topic sentence for the following paragraph. Then select three sentences to fit in the outline.*

TS:_____

1._____

2. Kathy is athletic.

3._____

4._____

Find answers to TEST YOURSELF on page 167.

FOUR WAYS TO POLISH YOUR SKILLS

Activity 35

In the following lists, circle the letter beside the sentence that does not develop the controlling idea which appears in the topic sentences. Then write out the paragraphs, leaving out sentences that do not belong.

1. TOPIC SENTENCE: I enjoy weekends.
   a. I can sleep late Saturday morning.
   b. My friends and I can visit and run around.
   c. I can do all kinds of shopping.
   d. School assignments are due on Monday.
   e. We usually go for a ride on Sunday afternoons.

_____

_____

_____

_____

_____

_____

_____

_____

_____

_____

2. TOPIC SENTENCE: Carlos is very interested in cars.

    a. He knows all the details about all the manufacturers' models.
    b. His parents allow him $5.50 a week for gas.
    c. He spends a lot of time each week making improvements on his old Ford.
    d. If there is a new-car exhibit in town, you will find him there.

_____

_____

_____

_____

_____

_____

_____

_____

_____

3. TOPIC SENTENCE: I easily give up doing my homework.

    a. I always start to feel hungry and go into the kitchen for a snack.
    b. I'll leave my studying to investigate any noise I hear.
    c. While I study, I try to listen to the radio with one ear.
    d. For me, physics is the hardest subject.
    e. I often leave my desk to go to the mirror to comb my hair.
    f. Often, in the middle of an assignment, I decide that my shoes need polishing and do that instead of the assignment in front of me.

_____

_____
_____
_____
_____
_____
_____
_____
_____
_____
_____
_____
_____
_____
_____
_____

4. TOPIC SENTENCE: The weather has been changeable.

   a. On Sunday we had a high wind that blew down some trees.
   b. Monday was so cold we had to turn on the heat and wear our winter coats.
   c. Tuesday we formed a group to go roller skating.
   d. By Wednesday the weather cleared and the sun came out.
   e. Thursday was as hot and humid as an August day.
   f. Friday morning it began to rain, and it looks as if we'll have a cold, steady wind for a few days.

_____
_____
_____
_____
_____

_____
_____
_____
_____
_____
_____
_____
_____
_____
_____
_____

5. TOPIC SENTENCE: All the people on our block give us trouble.
   a. Mrs. Brown calls the police whenever we want to play ball on the street.
   b. Mrs. Gonzales invites us in for lemonade every day.
   c. If we happen to stray into Mr. Hardy's yard, he yells at us.
   d. Mrs. Johnson complains that skateboarding makes too much noise.
   e. Yesterday Mr. Chan kept the Frisbee when it landed on his front porch.

_____
_____
_____
_____
_____
_____
_____

_____

_____

_____

_____

_____

_____

6. TOPIC SENTENCE: We had a hard time getting Peter out of the hole he had fallen into.

   a. First, we made a rope by linking our belts together.
   b. Then we lowered it to Peter, telling him to grasp the end.
   c. After he had hold of the belt-rope, we began to pull him slowly out of the hole.
   d. As he came up, no one dared to speak a word.
   e. The sides of the hole were covered with moss.
   f. Finally, we could grasp his arms, and, with a sigh of relief, we pulled him out onto the grassy bank.

_____

_____

_____

_____

_____

_____

_____

_____

_____

_____

_____

_____

_____

_____

_____

7. TOPIC SENTENCE: Summer vacation always seems short.
   a. On the last day of school, it seems that the three-month vacation will last forever.
   b. I wake up on the Fourth of July to find that I haven't really begun any of the things I'd planned to do.
   c. By August 2, my birthday, I feel that there isn't any time left at all.
   d. On Labor Day, just before school is to start again, I wonder where summer could have gone.
   e. It's always fun to have a reunion with my classmates on the first day of school.

_____

_____

_____

_____

_____

_____

_____

_____

_____

_____

_____

_____

_____

_____

8. TOPIC SENTENCE: Different cultural groups in Hawaii organize holiday celebrations in different ways.

   a. The Japanese, Chinese, and Koreans celebrate the coming of a new year by setting off firecrackers, Roman candles, sparklers, tiny rockets, and aerial lights.
   b. The Filipinos have their own celebrations with music and dance exhibitions and Filipino food, such as *kakanin* ("pastries") and *sabao* ("soup").
   c. Mainlanders like to stroll down Kalakaua Avenue in Honolulu during the warm evenings.
   d. Native Hawaiians gather to eat at a typical luau, sampling *poi, lau lau*, wild pig, *lome lome*, salmon, *opihi*, raw fish, and other Hawaiian favorites.

_____

_____

_____

_____

_____

_____

_____

_____

_____

_____

_____

_____

_____

_____

_____

_____

_____

_____

_____

_____

9. TOPIC SENTENCE: It is hard to travel to work by bus during the rush hour.

a. You have to wait in long lines at the bus stop.
b. When the bus arrives, someone always tries to push past you to get in first.
c. After you pay your fare, you are shoved down the aisle by the rest of the boarding passengers.
d. Sometimes you can read the morning newspaper during the ride.
e. A passenger standing next to you might shove his or her elbow in your ribs, step on your toes, or even drop cigarette ashes on you.
f. It certainly is a relief when you finally reach your stop.

_____

_____

_____

_____

_____

_____

_____

_____

_____

_____

_____

_____

_____

_____

_____

_____

_____

_____

10. TOPIC SENTENCE: You should not trust advertisements.

   a. Read advertisements.

   b. Look at the products themselves to see if they really are what the advertisers claim them to be.

   c. Talk to your friends to find out if they have had success with the products.

   d. Switch channels if a television program is interrupted by too many commercials.

   e. Read about product research in *Consumer Reports*.

   f. Above all, don't buy a product because an advertisement says that a famous football player or a movie star likes it.

_____

_____

_____

_____

_____

_____

_____

_____

_____

_____

_____

_____

_____

_____

_____

_____

_____

_____

_____

Activity 36

Some of the following paragraphs are not unified because they contain sentences that do not relate to the controlling idea. If you find such a sentence, underline it. Then write out each paragraph, leaving out any sentence you have underlined.

1. Because a sprained ankle offers all the benefits of an illness and few of the disadvantages, it is a very popular complaint. It never kills anyone, and it always gets better in a short time. It brings sympathy and is a reason for a week's absence from school. The dean checks into unauthorized absences. Since there is usually no pain except when the ankle is moved, it gives its victims a perfect rest and a delightful reason to be waited on.

_____

_____

_____

_____

_____

_____

_____

_____

_____

_____

_____

_____

2. Truly, nylon is a magic word. First, it is a mystery of chemistry. Second, it is made by what seems like a sleight-of-hand process. Third, it has many artful uses. Fourth, cotton is not as heavy as wool. Fifth, the future uses of nylon may cause as much surprise as the sight of a white rabbit being pulled out of a magician's hat. Nylon is a miracle of modern science.

_____

_____

_____

_____

_____

_____

_____

_____

_____

_____

_____

_____

_____

3. The discovery of America was an accident. It was the result of Europe's desire for trade with China and India. In 1492, Christopher Columbus set out under the flag of Spain to find a direct sea route to the rich trading areas of the Far East. He hoped to find a shorter route to China and India. So he sailed due west across the Atlantic. Instead, he found two huge continents that were until then unknown to Europe. They blocked his way to the Far East. These two continents were North America and South America.

_____

_____

_____

_____

_____
_____
_____
_____
_____
_____
_____
_____
_____
_____
_____
_____
_____
_____

4. Since drug addiction is an emotional problem, an antiaddiction program that works well for the British might not work so well with people of a different culture. To support this view, authorities point to the drug problem in Hong Kong. Shopping bargains are easy to find in this free port. Hong Kong is a British colony. It enjoys the benefits of the "British system." But Hong Kong, with one third the population of New York City, has more addicts (about 150,000, or one for every 10 adult males) than are found in the entire United States. In fact, Hong Kong is the only city in the world with more heroin addicts than New York.

_____
_____
_____
_____
_____

_____

_____

_____

_____

_____

_____

_____

_____

_____

_____

_____

_____

_____

_____

_____

_____

_____

_____

_____

5. Mount Lassen, 10,453 feet high, is one of the most active volcanoes in the United States. It had strong eruptions in 1914–1917 and minor activity as late as 1921. Gold was first discovered in California in 1849. Nature has softened down most of the rough spots on Mount Lassen's slopes, softening them with vegetation. But it is still a place of jagged cliffs, bubbling mud pots, fuming vents, boiling lakes, and weird lava formations. Although volcano activity in Hawaii has been more spectacular recently, California's Mount Lassen might erupt at any time.

_____

_____

_____

_____

_____

_____

_____

_____

_____

_____

_____

_____

_____

_____

_____

_____

_____

_____

6. People think of the United States as a rich and plentiful nation. It is, but it is not self-sufficient. Its reliance on foreign sources is made clear every day in the year. Topping the list is oil. Most oil is imported from the Middle Eastern countries of Saudi Arabia and Iran. Or take sugar: cane sugar ranks high in value among imported foodstuffs. Or consider coffee. Coffee drinking could not be an American habit if imports from Venezuela and Brazil were cut off. Morning readers would not have their newspapers without printing ink. Much of that comes from Canada. The chief source of raw silk is Japan. A wristwatch may or may not be a Swiss watch, but the inner movements are probably imported. Ninety percent of them are.

_____

_____

_____

_____

_____

_____

_____

_____

_____

_____

_____

_____

_____

_____

_____

_____

_____

_____

_____

_____

_____

_____

_____

_____

_____

7. Learning a foreign language has changed. Not so long ago, students
   would sit with pens in hand, writing the basic forms of a language,
   learning structures they would never be able to speak. In that same
   classroom today, pens and notebooks have been put away. The spo-
   ken sounds of foreign tongue fill the room. Today the last skill

learned — writing a foreign language — comes as a natural and possible part of the total language-learning process. Yet, just a few years ago, the last skill learned was the first skill mastered today — speaking a foreign tongue. To visit some foreign countries, travelers have to apply for visas.

_____

_____

_____

_____

_____

_____

_____

_____

_____

_____

_____

_____

_____

_____

_____

_____

_____

_____

_____

_____

_____

_____

8. Desert animals have the problem of finding water and keeping it. Phoenix gets much of its water from the Colorado River. Insect-eaters draw liquid from their foods. Most desert animals avoid the

drying heat as much as possible. They spend their time in burrows where the damp earth and coolness cut down the amount of evaporation from their breathing. All birds seek shade wherever they can find it. Reptiles have an added reason for avoiding the desert sun's rays. Being coldblooded creatures without the protection of fur, feathers, or other cooling devices, snakes can be killed by a short exposure to full sun. Many desert animals find an important source of water through the breakdown of fats in the body. Lizards, for example, store fat in their tails, much as the camel stores fat in his hump.

_____

_____

_____

_____

_____

_____

_____

9. Some teachers seem to be good teachers. But they are not, even though their students have no special fault to find with them. They are not good teachers because they have no social vision, no social urge, no fight. They know their respective fields well. They have orderly minds. Their courses are well planned and efficiently taught. Yet something keeps them from being a great teacher like Socrates. This kind of teacher is more interested in the subject being taught than in students or social progress. A good teacher never ceases to think of the fates and sorrows of fellow beings. A good teacher is always eager to bring about a social structure in which people will be free to be themselves. European countries seem to accept individuality much more than the United States does.

_____

_____

_____

_____

_____

_____

_____

_____

_____

_____

_____

_____

_____

_____

_____

_____

_____

_____

_____

_____

_____

_____

10. Of the many ways to measure body temperature, the most common is the mercury thermometer. A mercury thermometer consists of a narrow, sealed glass tube called a capillary. At the bottom end is a small bulb. Mercury fills the bulb and the bottom part of the capillary; the remaining section is empty. The thermometer works on this principle: when the temperature rises, the mercury and the glass bulb both expand. But the mercury expands more than the glass does. This forces a small part of the mercury up the narrow capillary. A scale is engraved on the glass to allow a person to read the temperature.

_____

_____

_____

_____

_____

_____

_____

_____

_____

_____

_____

_____

_____

_____

_____

_____

_____

Activity 37

Use three of the sentences below as beginning topic sentences to write three short, unified paragraphs.

1. Many different types of popular music are popular with record buyers.
2. Anyone who cooks needs to develop kitchen shortcuts.
3. I have a plan for what would be an ideal art class.
4. People can show their respect for nature in many different ways.
5. Young people strongly feel the need for their parents to treat them consistently.
6. When students are bored, they develop certain clock-watching techniques.
7. Newspaper columnists and features make reading a newspaper enjoyable.

Paragraph 1: _____

_____

_____

_____

_____

_____

_____

_____

_____

_____

_____

_____

_____

_____

_____

_____

_____

_____

_____

_____

_____

Paragraph 2: _____

_____

_____

_____

_____

_____

_____

_____

_____

_____

_____

_____

_____

_____

_____

_____

_____

_____

_____

_____

_____

_____

_____

Paragraph 3: _____

_____

_____

_____

_____

_____

_____

_____

_____

_____

_____

_____

_____

_____

_____

_____

_____

_____

_____

_____

_____

_____

_____

_____

Activity 38

Write a paragraph on any subject as an example of unity. Include a topic sentence in any position in the paragraph. Make sure that the topic sentence contains a controlling idea. Develop your paragraph only with sentences that relate to the controlling idea.

_____

_____

_____

ANSWERS to TEST YOURSELF

Paragraph 1.	Paragraph 2.
TS: Kathy is athletic	TS: d
1. b	1. a
2. c	2. Kathy is athletic.
3. f	3. e
4. h	4. g

UNITY POST-TEST

Find the sentence that does not fit logically into the paragraph. Then write it out on the lines that follow.

Television programming in the United States has become increasingly monotonous. One year, half of the evening television programs will be westerns. The next year, they will be detective shows. Sex and violence are stressed in show after show. The New York theater is also in a decline. The advertisers who pay huge sums of money for television time are responsible for television's weak programming. Advertisers believe that they cannot afford to experiment with original and creative shows. Time after time, they choose what they think will be a "sure thing." In their minds, profits are the first concern. Quality of programming takes a second place.

_____

_____

_____

7 COHERENCE

Riding a direct line through the surf without falling is a surfer's goal. A writer is also concerned with direct forward movement. By creating a direct line of thought, a writer gives a paragraph its necessary coherence.

COHERENCE PRE-TEST

1) If the idea in the second sentence logically follows the idea in the first sentence, place a (+) on the line at the right. If the idea in the second sentence does not logically follow the idea in the first sentence, place a (−) on the line at right. The first one is done for you.

EXAMPLE: Mollie filled out a form at the employment agency.
     She was hoping to find a job.   +

 1. The dormitory was clean
   There was dust under the beds.   −

 2. Juan never goes out on weeknights.
   He went to the movies Thursday.   _____

3. Something kept Doris awake.
   A tree was shaking in the wind.   _____

4. Ellen listened closely to Mrs. Rodriguez.
   She was interested in what her lawyer had to say.   _____

5. I pulled off my shirt and pants.
   I tied my necktie.   _____

6. Robert was running gracefully.
   His legs were skimming over the track.   _____

7. Maria turned off the light.
   She read another chapter of the book.   _____

8. The boat moved away from the dock.
   The captain ordered the crew to raise the anchor.   _____

9. Manuel was lost in Boston.
   His suitcase felt heavy in his hands.   _____

10. Many people give too much importance to appearance.
    They like other people for their minds.   _____

2) Add a second sentence that contains an idea which logically follows the
   idea in the first sentence. The first one is done for you.

   EXAMPLE: Sarah only likes to see one movie at a time.
                We didn't go to the double feature.

   1. It was a stormy day.
      There was rain and hail.

   2. Madeline was badly frightened.

   _____

   _____

   _____

   3. My sister is conceited.

   _____

   _____

   _____

4. I ran to the mailbox.

_____

_____

5. Eve opened the box of chocolates.

_____

_____

6. The governor made a speech.

_____

_____

7. The customs official told Isabel to close her suitcase.

_____

_____

8. Professor Eckhart is doing important research.

_____

_____

9. Anita returned the ice skates.

_____

_____

10. A diving crew is looking for treasure in a sunken ship.

_____

_____

_____

What is **coherence** in writing? Coherence in writing means that each sentence in a paragraph naturally leads to the next sentence in explaining the controlling idea. A writer is like a pianist who hopes to play a composition from beginning to end without stopping. A writer does not want to stop speaking to his or her reader until the point of a paragraph is made. So a writer tries to move smoothly from sentence to sentence in presenting a paragraph's main idea. Coherence is unbroken forward movement — a mark of successful English writing.

To gain coherence, many writers decide before writing how they will build each paragraph. There are many possibilities. A paragraph can grow from the least important example to the most important example, or from the most important example to the least important one. It can develop chronologically (in time order), spatially (in space order), inductively (from specific facts to a general conclusion), or deductively (from a general conclusion to specific facts).

Each of these six ways to build paragraphs helps to improve writing. Let us look at examples.

1. Development from least important to most important example

An author has many different ways to show what a character is like. Certain hand movements, ways of speaking, or style of dress tell some things about a character. Other characters may talk about the character, or the author may even make revealing comments. How a character reacts to something done to him or her is also important. But the most information comes from what a character says and from what a character does.

After the opening topic sentence, the writer gives some *less* important examples of the controlling idea "different ways." Not until three sentences later, in the paragraph's last sentence, does the writer name the *most* important ways an author can show what a character is like — by what a character says and what a character does.

2. Development from most important to least important example

Savita likes living in a private house better than in a dormitory for a number of reasons. First, it costs less. For example, she paid $120 a month to live in a dorm, but it costs her only $90 to live in a private home. Second, she has more privacy in a home. In a dorm, she shared a room with another girl, but in a home, she has a room all to herself. Third, it is easier to study in a private home. A dorm is often too noisy, but a home rarely is. Finally, she can keep her car at a house. At campus dorms, there are no parking spaces for student cars. For these reasons, Savita likes to live off-campus.

Immediately following the opening topic sentence, the writer names the most important reason for Savita's liking to live in a private house: it costs less. The next three reasons she gives as the paragraph draws to a close are increasingly less important.

3. Development by time (chronologically)

First, pre-heat, cool, and weigh a clean, dry Pyrex test tube on a chemical balance to the nearest O. Olg. Next, record the mass in the Data Table on the following page. Use a platform balance to weigh out approximately 1.5 g. of C.P. grade copper (II) oxide. Then transfer it to the weighed Pyrex tube. Now reweigh the tube and contents to the nearest O. Olg. Do not forget to record the mass as before.

In this paragraph describing the process of scientific measurement, all six sentences follow each other in time. The steps of the process are arranged in the order in which they actually happen.

4. Development by space (spatially)

Carlos looked at the scene from the summit of Mt. Everest. In the distant north he saw Tibet. A bit closer, he saw some of the lower peaks of the Himalayan range. On a ledge about one thousand feet below him, he saw the figures of some of the men who had helped him prepare for his final climb to the top.

One way to organize spatially is to begin with an object that is farthest away from a viewer and then in each sentence move gradually closer to the point where the viewer is standing. Following the opening topic sentence of this paragraph, the three sentences do this.

5. Development from specific facts to generalization (inductively)

Give students a chance to grow. Do not mold them from one of a thousand patterns. Let them seek knowledge, but do not find it for them. Let them learn patience; do not force it on them. Let them take their own time to grow; do not set rigid time schedules. Most of all, do not push them against a stone wall, crushing them with knowledge gained from the experience of others. Experience cannot be taught; it must come slowly through personal search.

The first six sentences of this paragraph give specific facts that lead up to the general conclusion in the closing sentence: "Experience cannot be taught; it must come slowly through personal search."

6. **Development from generalization to specific facts (deductively)**

> Solitude can be a state of loneliness, or it can be a state of sweetness and contentment. It can be avoided fearfully, or it can be accepted gratefully. It can hurt a life, or it can help a life. Solitude is part of everyone's life. How much wiser is that person who makes a friend of solitude rather than an enemy, that person who welcomes moments alone because they help in the crucial process of self-discovery.

"Solitude can be a state of loneliness, or it can be a state of sweetness and contentment." is this paragraph's opening topic sentence. It also states a generalization. It is followed by four sentences that explain in specific terms the meaning of the opening statement.

TEST YOURSELF

The following paragraph tells how to build a fire, but its sentences are out of order. List the proper order by number. Then rewrite the paragraph so the directions are clear.

(1) When you want to build a fire, the first thing to do is to get some logs, some kindling, and some paper. (2) Then strike a match. (3) Be sure to arrange the logs closely together on top of the kindling before you light the paper. (4) After wadding up the paper, put it on the ground and scatter the kindling on it.

_____

_____

_____

_____

_____

_____

_____

_____

_____

_____

Find answers to TEST YOURSELF on page 191.

FOUR WAYS TO POLISH YOUR SKILLS

Activity 39

Revise the lettering of the following sentences so that this new order will form a coherent paragraph. Then write out the paragraph on the lines below.

1.

___a. When he was almost at the top, his foot had slipped on a loose rock, and he had nearly fallen a thousand feet down the steep side of the peak.

___b. At the bottom, Professor John Mathewson had sprained his ankle.

___c. Finally, Professor John Mathewson crawled to the top of Mount Everest.

___d. It had been a long, hard climb to the top.

___e. Part way up, he had lost his rope.

_____

_____

_____

_____

_____

_____

_____

_____

_____

_____

_____

_____

2.

___a. Then, too, my mother wanted me to stay close to my sister.

___b. I argued that two years of study abroad would help me a lot at this stage of my career.

___c. For one thing, my father was not well.

___d. Finally my sister offered to stay at home alone during my absence.

___e. I found it hard to leave my home and travel to another land.

___ f. This made some of my problems begin to vanish.

_____

_____

_____

_____

_____

_____

_____

_____

_____

3.

___a. Behind the house a hill rose sharply.

___b. Standing at the edge of the road, I looked up the gently winding driveway that climbed to the front of the house.

___c. I had never seen such a lovely setting for a house.

___d. The hill ended in a curved peak that seemed to frame the whole scene.

___e. The house stood on a level space surrounded by tall oak trees.

_____

_____

_____

_____

_____

_____

_____

_____

_____

_____

_____

_____

_____

4.

___a. He spent the first fifteen minutes of the hour working on the first of ten examination problems.

___b. He spent other minutes doodling on his test paper.

___c. José did not complete his mathematics examination yesterday.

___d. Like many college students, he does not know how to use time profitably during an examination.

_____

_____

_____

_____

_____

_____

_____

_____

_____

_____

_____

_____

_____

5.

    ___a. Then you will come to a hallway leading to the library's music room.

    ___b. Walking around the information desk to the left, you will pass a children's reading room on your right.

    ___c. The sign reads, To the Music Room.

    ___d. As you enter the main door of the library, you will see the information desk directly in front of you.

    ___e. At the end of the hallway you will see a sign.

_____

_____

_____

_____

_____

_____

_____

_____

_____

_____

_____

_____

_____

_____

_____

6.

    ___a. In the late 1920s, propeller airplanes began to fly at speeds of more than 100 miles an hour.

    ___b. When the wheel was invented over a thousand years ago, man learned that it was possible to travel faster on wheels than on foot.

___c. With the invention of the steam engine about two hundred years ago, man began to travel at what was called "dangerous" speeds of between 20 to 30 miles an hour.

___d. Man has learned to travel faster and faster throughout history.

___e. About twenty years ago, man began to travel in commercial jet planes at speeds above 500 miles an hour.

___f. The gasoline engines that were used between 1900 and 1920 developed speeds up to 60 miles an hour.

_____

_____

_____

_____

_____

_____

_____

_____

_____

_____

_____

_____

_____

_____

_____

_____

_____

_____

_____

_____

7.

___a. Later, as people began to multipy and move, they began to change in physical appearance.

___b. The Caucasians are identified with Europe; the Negroes, with Africa; and the Mongolians, with Asia.

___c. Human beings populated a large part of the planet Earth.

___d. Will all people someday belong to one group?

___e. Yet, at one time, the number of people was small and probably limited to one part of the globe, like Central Asia or possibly Africa.

___f. Today, however, the groups are constantly mixing and spreading to all parts of the world.

___g. In fact, the number of people has grown so rapidly in recent years that we may need to find new places to settle.

___h. Scientists say that originally humans may all have been the same.

___i. Is it possible that our future will be like our past?

___j. Three major groups appeared, the Caucasian, the Negro, and the Mongolian.

___k. Each group had its home area.

_____

_____

_____

_____

_____

_____

_____

_____

_____

_____

_____

_____

_____

_____

_____

_____

_____

_____

_____

_____

_____

_____

_____

_____

_____

_____

_____

_____

_____

_____

Activity 40

Some of the following paragraphs lack coherence. Rewrite any faulty paragraphs, changing the order of sentences to make them coherent.

1. Second, she never missed a class. Elizabeth's classmates knew that she would win the top award in chemistry during her senior year at Columbia University. Third, she performed every required experiment in all her chemistry courses. First, she had studied chemistry during her sophomore and junior years. Fourth, she always worked hard.

_____

_____

_____

_____

_____

_____

_____

_____

_____

_____

_____

2. While standing in front of the information desk in the library, I saw some students using the files in the reference room some distance away. About fifteen feet away from me, an old lady wearing a large red hat put on her glasses. She was studying a rare book in one of the locked display cases. Much closer to me, two students were quietly but seriously talking about a book.

_____

_____

_____

_____

_____

_____

_____

_____

_____

_____

3. I had a terrible morning today. In the middle of a class, I discovered I had left my physics assignments in my locker. I tripped over a curb on my way to my political science class and tore my raincoat. At the end of the class, the professor would not let me go to lunch on time. I slept so late that I did not have time to eat any breakfast. I had not turned in my assignments, and he wanted to talk over this problem with me.

_____

_____

---

4. Our candidates do not want our blessings. When she went to the polls, she took her ballot and simply wrote on the bottom of it, "God bless you all!" We should not be like the lady who knew all the candidates in a small-town election and thought they were all such nice people that she could not choose among them. They want our votes. We must all use our right to vote.

---

5. But the state's population, although it is growing at a tremendous rate, is well below that of the city of Pittsburgh. Arizona is a large state. Yet Arizona could absorb all six New England states, add Hol-

land, and still have more than enough room to tuck in Switzerland. Arizonans have plenty of living room. It is only 638,000. On a map, bordered by other western states, Arizona appears to be only of average size.

_____

_____

_____

_____

_____

_____

_____

_____

_____

_____

6. Why not start now? Use it correctly in conversation three times before tomorrow's class. A good vocabulary, then, can give you a real sense of power and a feeling of pleasure. The word will then be yours to keep. You'll be on your way toward making yourself a master of words. If you learn a new word every day, in a year's time you will have 365 new sources of power and pleasure. Look up the word *genial* in a dictionary before you leave school this afternoon.

_____

_____

_____

_____

_____

_____

_____

_____

_____

_____

_____

_____

_____

Activity 41

Use three of the following sentences as beginning topic sentences to write three short, coherent paragraphs.

1. It is not a good idea to go grocery shopping when you are hungry.
2. Getting a driver's license is a complicated process.
3. Clothing styles change from one country to another.
4. An athlete in training needs to show much self-discipline.
5. Students have different ways of providing themselves with transportation.
6. Buying on credit has both advantages and disadvantages.

Paragraph 1: _____

_____

_____

_____

_____

_____

_____

_____

_____

_____

_____

_____

_____

_____

_____

_____

_____

_____

_____

_____

Paragraph 2: _____

_____

_____

_____

_____

_____

_____

_____

_____

_____

_____

_____

_____

_____

_____

_____

_____

_____

_____

_____

_____

_____

_____

Paragraph 3: _____

_____

_____

_____

_____

_____

_____

_____

_____

_____

_____

_____

_____

_____

_____

_____

_____

_____

_____

_____

_____

Activity 42

Write a paragraph on any subject as an example of coherence. Include a topic sentence in any position in the paragraph. Make sure the topic sentence contains a controlling idea.

_____

_____

_____

_____

_____

_____

_____

_____

_____

_____

_____

_____

_____

_____

_____

_____

_____

_____

_____

_____

_____

_____

_____

_____

_____

_____

_____

_____

_____

ANSWERS to TEST YOURSELF   1
                                 4
                                 3
                                 2

COHERENCE POST-TEST

The fourteen sentences in this paragraph are in the wrong order. (1) List sentences by number in the correct order to form a coherent paragraph. (2) Write out the revised paragraph.

(1) The Golden Gate Bridge separates San Francisco Bay from the Pacific Ocean. (2) She went to Japan Center, where the buildings and restaurants looked familiar. (3) But San Francisco did not look anything like New York. (4) It crosses from San Francisco to Oakland. (5) Many homes have views of the bay and ocean. (6) Here she was able to talk with people in her native language. (7) She expected to find the tall skyscrapers she had seen on postcards of New York. (8) The Bay Bridge is majestic. (9) Miyoko's first stop on her flight from Tokyo to the United States was San Francisco. (10) Miyoko especially liked the two bridges that cross San Francisco Bay. (11) From them she learned that San Francisco is a most hospitable city for people from the Orient. (12) After seeing the many hills and bridges, Miyoko was surprised to learn that San Francisco has a very large Japanese population. (13) Even more beautiful is the Golden Gate Bridge, stretching from San Francisco to Marin County. (14) For one thing, it is all built on hills.

1. _____
2. _____
3. _____
4. _____
5. _____
6. _____
7. _____
8. _____
9. _____
10. _____
11. _____
12. _____
13. _____
14. _____

_____

_____

_____

PARAGRAPH WRITING POST-TEST

1. Study this paragraph to see if it has the elements that a paragraph should contain: topic sentence, controlling idea, unity, coherence, transitions, subordination, and parallelism. Write out specific examples of the topic sentence, controlling idea, subordination, and parallelism. List transitions. In a short paragraph, explain why the paragraph does or does not have unity and coherence.

Shopping habits in the United States have changed greatly in the last quarter of the twentieth century. Early in the 1900s, most American towns and cities had a Main Street. Main Street was always in the heart of a town. This street was lined on both sides with many varied businesses. Here, shoppers walked into stores to look at all sorts of merchandise: clothing, furniture, hardware, groceries. In addition, some shops offered services. These shops included drugstores, restaurants, shoe-repair stores, and barber or hairdressing shops. But in the 1950s, a change began to take place. Too many automobiles had crowded into Main Street. Too few parking places were available to shoppers. Because the streets were crowded, merchants began to look with interest at the open spaces outside the city limits. Open space is what their car-driving customers needed. And open space is what they got when the first shopping center was built. Shopping centers, or malls, started as a collection of small new stores built away from congested city centers. Attracted by hundreds of free parking spaces, customers were drawn away from downtown areas to the outlying malls. And the growing popularity of shopping centers led in turn to the building of bigger and better-stocked stores. By the late 1970s, many shopping malls had almost developed into small cities themselves. In addition to providing the convenience of one-stop shopping, malls were transformed into landscaped parks, with benches, fountains, and outdoor entertainment. For example, one of the most spectacular shopping malls is The Galleria in Houston, Texas. Inside the Galleria, dozens of shops face balconies that rise for several stories above a floor-level indoor ice skating rink. Some of Houston's best restaurants are also here. Atop the whole mammoth structure is a soaring new hotel. The Galleria, and other imaginative shopping centers throughout the United States, have led a magazine to title its recent leading article "The Malling of America."

Topic sentence: _____

_____

_____

Controlling idea: _____

_____

Subordination: _____

_____

195

_____

_____

_____

_____

_____

_____

Parallelism: _____

_____

_____

_____

_____

_____

_____

Transitions: _____

_____

_____

Unity and coherence: _____

_____

_____

_____

_____

_____

_____

_____

_____

_____

_____

_____

_____

2. Think up a topic sentence with a controlling idea on a subject that interests you. Then develop a paragraph of at least eight sentences from your topic sentence.

_____

_____

_____

_____

_____

_____

_____

_____

_____

_____

_____

_____

_____

_____

_____

_____

_____

_____

_____

_____

_____

_____

_____

APPENDIX 1
Glossary of Terms Used in This Book

ADJECTIVE   One of the parts of speech. An adjective modifies (describes or limits) a noun or pronoun.

a **yellow** car, a **warm** day, an **angry** man

ADJECTIVE CLAUSE   A clause (group of words with a subject and predicate) used as an adjective to modify a noun or pronoun.

The woman **who was invited** could not come.
(The clause "who was invited" modifies the noun "woman.")

ADVERB   One of the parts of speech. An adverb modifies verbs, adjectives, and other adverbs.

She ran **fast.** (The adverb "fast" modifies the verb "ran.")
That suit is **very** attractive. (The adverb "very" modifies the adjective "attractive.")
That lock needs to fasten the door **more** firmly.
(The adverb "more" modifies the adverb "firmly.")

ADVERB CLAUSE   A clause used as an adverb to modify any part of speech that an adverb might modify, usually a verb. An adverb clause usually tells how, when, where, or why.

Life begins to be interesting **when you enroll in college.**
(The adverb clause "when you enroll in college" modifies the verb "begins.")

APPOSITIVE   A word placed next to a noun, used in the same way grammatically, and referring to the same person or thing.

Rodrigo, **our class president,** made a speech. (The appositive "our class president" renames the noun "Rodrigo" in different words.)

ARTICLE   Any of three words — **a, an,** and **the.**

A letter came for your today.
Katherine brought me **an** ice cream cone.
I sent **the** package by airmail.

BOLDFACE   This is a kind of type that is darker and thicker than the normal type found in a book. It is used to emphasize words: **boldface.**

CAUSE AND EFFECT.   A cause is a happening or act that produces an effect, or result. For example, lighting a fire in a fireplace can be the cause of raising the temperature in a room. The fire is the **cause;** the higher heat is the **effect.**

CHRONOLOGICAL   Chronological development means putting events in the order in which they happened in time. For example, the chronological order of a person's life would be birth, childhood, adolescence, youth, middle age, old age, death.

CLAUSE   A group of related words that contains a subject and a predicate. There are two kinds of clauses: main and subordinate. At least one main clause is necessary in any complete sentence. (A main clause makes an independent statement.) Subordinate clauses cannot stand alone as sentences.

MAIN CLAUSE: **The climate is delightful.**
SUBORDINATE   The band stopped playing **after you left.**
CLAUSE:

CLIMAX   A climax is a peak of importance. In writing, the term means saving your most important point to discuss last.

COHERENCE   Coherence is the straight line of development within a paragraph or composition. An English paragraph is coherent when its ideas are clearly related to each other in an orderly sequence. Each sentence in a coherent paragraph naturally grows out of each earlier sentence in developing the central idea.

COMPARISON   When you create a comparison, you put together situations, persons, or objects that are *alike* or *similiar* in their qualities. For example, the intense training of an athlete could be compared with the intense training of a ballet dancer.

CONCEDE (CONCESSION)   To concede (or make a concession) is to yield in favor of another point of view. In writing, subordinating words of concession, such as **although, unless, if,** and **than,** all introduce statements that qualify other statements in a sentence.

CONJUNCTION   One of the parts of speech. See Coordinating Conjunctions and Correlative Conjunctions.

CONSEQUENCE   Consequence is the result of an action. It is the relation of an effect to its cause. For example, for a car to run off the road could be the consequence of a driver letting go of the steering wheel.

CONTRAST   When you create a contrast, you put together situations, persons, or objects that are *unlike* or *dissimilar* in their qualities. For example, a pineapple could be contrasted with a squash.

CONTROLLING IDEA   The word or word group in a topic sentence that states the chief point that will be developed in a paragraph. In the following topic sentence, the words that express the controlling idea are boldfaced:

You can buy **many different kinds** of greeting cards.

COORDINATING CONJUNCTIONS   These are joining words used to connect words, phrases, or clauses that are equal in grammatical rank. The coordinating conjunctions are **and, but, or nor,** and **for.** Coordinating conjunctions are often used to join the two main clauses of a compound sentence:

First I shopped, **and** then I ate lunch.
I like your plan, **but** I have a few suggestions.

CORRELATIVE CONJUNCTIONS   These are joining words *used in pairs* to join grammatical elements of equal rank. Among the most common correlative conjunctions are **either . . . or, neither . . . nor, not only . . . but also, both . . . and**, and **whether . . . or.**

Martha wanted **either** a sweater **or** a blouse.
They wanted **both** a summer vacation **and** a winter vacation.

DANGLING PARTICIPLE   A participle or participial phrase dangles if the subject of the sentence is not the proper word for it to modify.

DANGLING: **Reading,** the *time* passed quickly.
                              (Is "time" reading?)

CORRECTED: **Reading,** *I* lost track of time.

DANGLING: **Giving a wrong answer,** a *blush* came on the student's face.
                              (Did the "blush" give the wrong answer?)

CORRECTED: **Giving a wrong answer,** the *student* blushed.

DEDUCTIVE   In logic, deduction is reasoning from the general to the particular. In writing, deductive development begins with a general statement and is followed by supporting facts or examples. For an example of deductive paragraph development, see page 176.

DEPENDENT CLAUSE   A dependent (or subordinate) clause is an incomplete unit of thought that needs to be attached to a main clause to make sense. Even though a dependent clause has a subject and predicate, it cannot stand alone. The dependent clause in the following sentence is boldfaced:

The company held a Christmas party for all employees **who work in the main building.**

EMPHASIS   Emphasis is special importance given to something. You can emphasize (or give added force) to an element in writing by using certain grammatical or punctuation forms. The boldfaced idea in the first sentence is emphasized by being placed in the main clause whereas the secondary idea appears in a dependent clause. The boldfaced words in the second sentence are emphasized by means of dashes.

Even though he was out of breath, **Mark blew out all the candles on his cake.**

They waited — **their arms covering their faces** — for the dynamite to explode.

GENERALIZATION   This is a broad, general statement that does not contain specific detail or supporting facts.

GERUND   A gerund is a verb form ending in **-ing.** It is not used as a verb, but as a noun.

GERUND AS SUBJECT:	**Jogging** is a popular exercise these days.
GERUND AS DIRECT OBJECT:	I like **sailing** on the bay.

GERUND PHRASE   A gerund phrase is a word group introduced by a gerund. (A phrase does not include a subject or predicate.)

Passing an examination is a satisfying experience.
He reached the mountaintop **by climbing all night.**

IMPLIED TOPIC SENTENCE   A paragraph can be written in which the topic sentence is not written out but is instead suggested by the other sentences developing the paragraph. When this happens, a paragraph is said to have an implied topic sentence. For an example of a paragraph with an implied topic sentence, see page 91.

INDUCTIVE   In logic, deduction is reasoning from the particular to the general. In writing, inductive development begins with supporting facts or examples that lead up to a general conclusion. For an example of inductive paragraph development, see page 175.

INFINITIVE   An infinitive is a verb form that is used after **to,** although sometimes the **to** is implied rather than expressed.

She tried **to call.**
Sam can **ice skate.**

INFINITIVE PHRASE   An infinitive phrase is a word group introduced by an infinitive. (A phrase does not include a subject or predicate.)

To put himself through college, he worked nights.
They studied the stock market **to protect their investments.**

ITALIC   This is a kind of type that slants to the right. It is used to set off titles of published works and to give special emphasis: *italic*.

LINKING   Several parts of speech provide linking (or joining) words. These include conjunctions (see Coordinating Conjunctions and Correlative Conjunctions), prepositions, and some verbs **(be, become, appear, seem, smell, taste,** and **feel).**

MAIN CLAUSE   (Sometimes called an "independent clause" or "principal clause.") A grammatical unit that contains a subject and a predicate and makes sense when it stands alone. A main clause is self-sufficient.

MAIN CLAUSE:	**The holidays are over.**
SUBORDINATE CLAUSE:	**She returned the book** after she had finished it.

MODIFIER.   A word, phrase, or clause used to describe, limit, or change the meaning of some other word, phrase, or clause.

WORD AS MODIFIER:	They returned the **broken** toy to the store.
PHRASE AS MODIFIER:	Sergio bought a ticket **for his brother.**
CLAUSE AS MODIFIER:	Let's wait **until the storm dies down.**

NOUN   One of the parts of speech. A noun is a word used to name a person, place, thing, or quality.

Gregory	**rabbit**	**engineer**
New York	**house**	**justice**

PARAGRAPH   A paragraph is a group of sentences that develops a single idea or unit of thought. (In rare cases, a single sentence can also act as a paragraph.) Each paragraph should leave a reader more informed at the end than at the beginning. A paragraph is usually indented a few spaces. This indentation tells a reader that the material presented in the paragraph represents a separate thought unit.

PARALLELISM   (Sometimes called "parallel structure" or "parallel forms.") Parallelism is the writing device of stating similar ideas by similar grammatical forms. Parallelism is a writer's technique of balancing like with like — nouns with nouns, participles with participles, prepositional phrases with prepositional phrases, and so forth.

Their favorite exercises are **jogging** and **bicycling.**
We hid the presents **in the kitchen** and **in the study.**
The real estate agent showed us one house **that was on the beach** and one house **that was on a hill.**

PARENTHESES   Parentheses are vertical, curved punctuation marks — ( ) — that are used to enclose figures within a sentence or to set off supplementary material.

> The chairman made two requests: (1) all members should be on time, and (2) the board should follow parliamentary procedure.
> When she finally talked (we could hardly hear her), she told us the reason she had been missing for two days.

PARTICIPLE   The present form of a verb ending in **-ing.** (Note that gerunds also have this ending.) The past participle usually ends in **-ed.** A participle may be used as the main element in a verb phrase or as an adjective.

PARTICIPLE AS VERB:	I am **asking** for a leave next year.
PRESENT PARTICI-PLE AS ADJECTIVE:	The **heating** element of my hair dryer has burned out.
PAST PARTICIPLE AS ADJECTIVE:	The house was newly **decorated.**

PARTICIPIAL PHRASE   A participial phrase is a word group introduced by a participle. (A phrase does not include a subject or predicate.)

> **Dancing across the room,** we became dizzy.
> They saw their friends **getting in the car.**

PHRASE   A group of related words that does not contain a subject and predicate. A phrase cannot stand alone as a sentence. There are several different kinds of phrases: prepositional phrases, participial phrases, adjective phrases, gerund phrases, infinitive phrases, verb phrases, and so forth. A phrase is named for the word that introduces it.

PREPOSITIONAL PHRASE:	We skated **on the lake.**
PARTICIPIAL PHRASE:	The man **sitting by the fire** is my uncle.
GERUND PHRASE:	**Running for student body president** is my goal.

PREPOSITION   One of the parts of speech. A preposition is used to introduce a noun or pronoun object and to link it to the rest of a sentence.

Sonia will arrive **at** noon **on** the plane **from** San Diego.

PREPOSITIONAL PHRASE   A prepositional phrase is a word group introduced by a preposition. (A phrase does not include a subject or predicate.)

They placed the gifts **under the Christmas tree.**

PRONOUN   One of the parts of speech. A pronoun is a word used in place of a noun. There are several kinds of pronouns: personal **(I, you, it, they)**; interrogative **(who, which, what)**; relative **(who, which, what, that)**; demonstrative **(this, that, these, those)**; indefinite **(each, either, anyone, few, none)**; reciprocal **(each other, one another)**; reflexive **(myself, yourself)**; and intensive **(myself, yourself, ourselves).**

QUALIFY   To qualify something in writing is to limit or restrict it by conditions or exceptions. The boldfaced statement in the sentence below is a qualifying one.

I will be glad to meet you at the track **although I will be about a half hour late.**

RELATIVE PRONOUN   One of four pronouns — **who, which, what,** or **that** — that introduces a relative clause. A relative pronoun acts as the subject of its clause.

The woman **who is taking flying lessons** will solo tomorrow.
He opened the letter **that came this morning.**

SENTENCE   A group of words that states a thought and contains a subject, either actual or implied, and a predicate. (A one-word verb with an understood subject is also considered a sentence: **Wait.**) There are four different sentence forms: **simple, compound, complex,** and **compound-complex.**

SIMPLE SENTENCE:	*This contains a single main clause.* Their car is new.
COMPOUND SENTENCE:	*This contains two or more main clauses.* Time was running out, and the project was still behind schedule.

COMPLEX
SENTENCE:

This contains one main clause and one or more dependent (or subordinate) clauses. The restaurant that opened yesterday serves Thai food.

COMPOUND-COM-
PLEX SENTENCE:

This contains two main clauses and one or more dependent clauses. The sun had set, and the rainstorm had begun before we reached home.

SERIES   Three or more words (or word groups) that are listed in sequence and have the same grammatical form.

We ate **bacon, eggs,** and **toast.**
Tom **shopped in the market, visited the museum,** and **toured the airplane factory.**

SPATIAL   Spatial development means writing about things in the order in which they appear in space. For example, in describing the main cities of Italy, a writer would either choose to move from north to south, beginning with Milan and ending with Naples, or to move from south to north. In a spatial development, a writer would not choose cities at random. Instead, a writer would move from north to south, left to right, below to above, or use whatever orderly spatial pattern suited the purpose of a paragraph.

SPECIFIC   Specific writing gives details and particular information about a subject. (The often-used terms *specific detail* and *concrete detail* mean the same thing.) Specific writing is the opposite of general writing. A generalization is a broad, overall statement that is supported by specific detail.

GENERALIZATION:
SPECIFIC DETAIL
ADDED:

West Germany produces high-quality cars.
West Germany produces such high-quality cars as **Porsche, BMW, and Mercedes-Benz.**

SUBORDINATION   The writing technique of combining two ideas that are unequal in importance so that a reader can quickly tell which idea is the central one. A writer creates subordination by placing the chief idea in a main clause and the less important idea in a dependent (or subordinate) clause.

MAIN IDEA   SUBORDINATE IDEA
Our house caught on fire   when the gas heater exploded.

SUBORDINATE CLAUSE   See Dependent Clause.

SYNONYM   A word that means the same thing (or almost the same thing) as another word. For example, "teacher" and "instructor" are synonyms. So are "sick" and "ill," "cheap" and "inexpensive," and "rich" and "wealthy."

TOPIC SENTENCE   A sentence that makes a limited statement about a subject. It usually contains a word or words that serve as a controlling idea to show the direction in which the paragraph will be developed. A topic sentence can appear anywhere in a paragraph, or it may not appear in a paragraph because its topic sentence is implied.

TRANSITIONS   Words or phrases that join one idea to another idea. A transition is used to draw a clearer relation between ideas. Transitions can more closely link both sentences and paragraphs.

Mike asked for a raise in salary. **It** was not granted.

UNITY   When a paragraph has unity, it states only a single thought. A unified paragraph presents only one topic or one part of a topic. All the facts, examples, and detail in the paragraph should explain this topic.

VERB   One of the parts of speech. A verb is a word or phrase that shows action, being, or state of being. Two categories of verbs are **transitive** and **intransitive.** A transitive verb takes an object (He bought **a tennis racquet.**); an intransitive verb does not take an object (The sun rises every morning). Some verbs may be either transitive or intransitive. "Cook" is an example (TRANSITIVE: Yesterday I cooked **a five-course meal.** INTRANSITIVE: Yesterday I cooked all afternoon.).

APPENDIX 2
Composition Topics

How to Pack a Suitcase
Renting an Apartment
My Favorite Amusement Park
A Special Hotel
Buying a Used Car

Restaurant Manners in the United States
Shopping in a Supermarket
How to Apply for a Job
Getting Around in a Big City
How to Pay Compliments

Roller Skating Is Good Exercise
The Many Services of a Bank
Body Surfing
Shopping for Clothes
Applying for a Driver's License

Training for an Athletic Team
An Appointment with a Doctor (Dentist)
Buying on Credit
Transportation Used by Students
Visiting a Discotheque

Learning to Sew
My Exercise Program
Collecting Records
Traveling on a Budget
Photography As a Hobby

Floors in a Building
Dressing for Different Occasions
The Concept of Time in the United States
Going on a Date
Foods I Can Do Without

Changing Clothing Styles
Kitchen Shortcuts
My Favorite Reading Materials
Formal and Informal Names
Planning a Vacation

Asking for Directions
Finding a Part-Time Job
Ways to Improve One's Looks
Holidays in the United States
Giving First Aid

How to Decorate a Room at Little Cost
Asking for Directions
Introducing Someone
Polite and Friendly Gestures in the United States
Places I Would Like to Visit Again

Taking Care of an Automobile
Developing Good Study Habits
How to Avoid Boredom
Developing a Healthy Self-Image
Why Blue Jeans Are Popular

APPENDIX 3
Forms for Writing Business Letters

There is a generally accepted form for writing a business letter in English, but the arrangement of parts within this form can vary. For instance, paragraphs in some business letters are indented. In other letters, paragraphs are written flush with the left margin. Optional, too, is the placement of the date in a business letter written on a piece of letterhead stationery. It can be centered, flush with the left margin, or flush right.

The form for business letters written on personal stationery differs from the form of letters written on company letterhead stationery. Compare the following examples, which show the two types of business letters you may expect to write:

BUSINESS LETTER ON PERSONAL STATIONERY

Note that, in this form, the two-line address of the letter writer and the one-line date are written in block form. They are set flush with the letter's right margin. The name, title, and address of the person being written to also appear in block form flush with the left margin. This information is spaced one line below the date line of the sender's address block at right. The writer has chosen to indent the paragraphs five spaces. The complimentary close begins on the center of the page, three or four spaces below the last line of the letter. The writer's name is typed three or four spaces below the complimentary close and aligned with it.

```
                                        284 Commonwealth Avenue
                                        Boston, Massachusetts 02115
                                        March 18, 1977

        Mr. Haskill L. Fisher
        Director of Admissions
        University of Southern California
        Los Angeles, California 90007

        Dear Mr. Fisher:

             Several of my friends who have studied at the University
        of Southern California's American Language Institute have
        recommended your school as a helpful place for intensive
        English language study.

             I am now enrolled as a sophomore at the Massachusetts
        Institute of Technology.  But I am thinking of transferring
        to the University of Southern California for my junior year.
        Can you tell me if I can enroll in a joint program in order
        to take some courses at the university while studying English
        at the American Language Institute?

             Please send me the forms and information necessary for
        me to apply for admission next year.

                                        Sincerely,

                                        Jamil Ambah

                                        Jamil Ambah
```

BUSINESS LETTER ON COMPANY STATIONERY

No sender's address block is necessary in this form because the information is contained in the printed letterhead. Here the date has been typed flush with the left margin, two spaces above the name and address of the person to whom the letter is being written. Note that paragraphs have been written in block form, not indented. The complimentary close is also written in block form and placed flush with the left margin, three or four spaces below the complimentary close.

Since the letter has been dictated to a secretary, the initials of the person dictating appear in capital letters, followed by a colon and the secretary's initials in lowercase letters. This information is placed flush with the left margin, several spaces below the complimentary close. Here is the meaning of the other symbols appearing in this position:

THE UNIVERSITY OF ARIZONA

TUCSON, ARIZONA 85721

COLLEGE OF AGRICULTURE

SCHOOL OF RENEWABLE NATURAL RESOURCES
325 BIOLOGICAL SCIENCES EAST BUILDING

12 October 1977

Mr. Sidney L. Hopper
Associate Editor
Atlas Books
18 River Street
Albany, New York 01385

Dear Mr. Hopper:

This is a quick answer to your letter of October 9. It is
written as I am leaving for the ASLA convention. Yes, I
would be very happy to work with you on the rewriting of the
Desert Gardening book. It will be a pleasantly creative
project to look forward to.

I don't think time will be a problem for me. But I should
mention that I have been working with a former graduate student
on a book she is writing on landscape plants for arid regions.
She has been working on it for several years. If it ever gets
finished, it probably will be published by the University of
Arizona Press. I don't think this will conflict in any way
with what you are doing, but I feel that I should call it to
your attention.

When I return from San Diego, I will write you again.

Very truly yours,

Arnold D. Bennett
Professor of Landscape Architecture

cc: Ruth Perrine
Encl. 2
ADB:mb

cc. Ruth Perrine — A carbon copy of the letter has been mailed to
Ruth Perrine.

Encl. 2 — Two enclosures have been sent along with the letter.
These might include such items as added pages of information, bro-
chures, photographs, or application forms.

ADB:mb — Writer's initials (ADB) and secretary's initials (mb).

APPENDIX 4
Phrasal Verbs

A phrasal verb, like an idiom, is an expression that is not easy to understand even if you know the meaning of its separate parts. Because such verbs often appear in both writing and speech, it is helpful to learn them and to have a reference source to refer to.

Phrasal verbs are often created by adding a preposition to a basic verb. Doing this changes the verb's meaning. For example, the verb *drop* means "to let something fall." But *drop in* means "to visit someone without having received an invitation," and *drop out* means "to give up doing what one usually does." You will find that many phrasal verbs have more than one meaning. For instance, *turn in* means "to give something to someone": (I **turned in** my test paper to the instructor). But the same phrase can also mean "to go to sleep": (Because it was past midnight, I decided to **turn in** for the night).

The grammatical and syntactical flexibility of phrasal verbs may sometimes puzzle you. For example, the two-word phrase *make up* can mean "to settle an argument with someone" (We will **make up** our differences today). Or it can mean "to apply cosmetics" (She **makes up** her face every morning). But when the two words are combined into one word, *makeup*, it becomes a noun meaning "cosmetics" (Her **makeup** was attractive). Many verbs combine with prepositions to form nouns, as in *checkup*, or adjectives, as in *well-to-do*.

Equally important, phrasal verbs can often be arranged in several different combinations, although certain combinations are not possible. For instance, *do over,* meaning "repeat," may be combined with a noun or pronoun in three ways:

do over the lesson/do the lesson over/do it over BUT NOT **do over it**

In the same way, *do without,* meaning "give up" or "forego," patterns like this:

do without money/do without it
BUT NOT **do money without/do it without**

Sometimes a difference in syntax, or word order, of a phrasal verb will result in opposite meanings. The meaning of *call on,* for example, depends on how it is combined with other words:

I **called on** him. *(I visited him.)*
I **called** him **on.** *(I challenged him to fight.)*

Following are twenty verbs, each followed by several phrasal verbs that are built from the basic verb. The phrasal verbs are first defined and then written in context. Many of these phrasal verbs have more than the six or seven meanings given here.

When a phrasal verb can be separated by having another word fit between its parts, the words *can be separated* appear following the phrasal verb. For example:

do over *(can be separated)*
The instructor asked me to **do over** the exercise.
He asked me to **do** it **over.**

1. Phrasal Verbs from **to do**

do away with: abolish   **have nothing to do with:** refrain
do over *(can be separated):*   from, avoid
   repeat   **outdo:** do better than, exceed
do without: give up, forego

The manufacturer wanted to **do away with** certain fringe benefits expected by his workers. He was annoyed that much of their work was careless and had to be **done over.** He decided that his employees could **do without** several paid holidays. But the workers' union would **have nothing to do with** the owner's plan. The union **outdid** itself in pleading the workers' case.

2. Phrasal Verbs from **to stand.**

take a stand: assume a position or attitude
stand by: be loyal to, support
stand for: tolerate, agree to

stand up to: offer resistance
stand out: be prominent
stand one up *(can be separated):* fail to appear

When asked to **take a stand** on civil rights, the politician announced that he would **stand by** his earlier position of strict observance of the laws. He said he would not **stand for** discrimination in housing or education. He promised to **stand up to** any attempts to repeal civil rights laws. Though he **stood out** as an outspoken liberal, the politician angered a group of newspaper reporters by **standing them up** at a scheduled press conference.

3. Phrasal Verbs from **to come**

come about: happen
come across: chance to meet
come down with: become sick with

come in handy: prove useful
come out: appear, be published
come through: succeed, arrive

It **came about** that the movie actress's visit to Mexico was ill-timed. In Guadalajara she **came across** a former husband whom she was unhappy to see. Then in Puerto Vallarta she **came down with** stomach flu. This was over in two days, though, because some medicine she had brought from Los Angeles **came in handy.** When news of her misadventures **came out** in the American newspapers, her agent was pleased because he felt that she had **come through** for him in keeping her name in the public eye.

4. Phrasal Verbs from **to turn**

turn in *(can be separated):* submit, deliver, go to sleep
turn down *(can be separated):* reject
turn off *(can be separated):* stop something from functioning

turn on *(can be separated):* start something functioning
turn out *(can be separated):* develop, gather
take turns: alternate in an activity
turn up: appear

Shortly after the writer **turned in** his short story to the magazine, he received a letter telling him that his work had been **turned down.** Hearing this, he **turned off** the television set, **turned on** the air conditioner,

-and began to **turn out** another story. For three days he **took turns** between writing and eating; then he mailed what he had written. This effort produced results: the second story **turned up** in the April issue of the magazine.

5. Phrasal Verbs from **to give**

> **give way:** retreat, collapse
> **give up** *(can be separated):* surrender
> **given to:** in the habit of
>
> **give out:** wear out, expire
> **give ground:** make a concession

In spring the rebelling faction first **gave way** to the government forces, and by winter the rebels finally **gave up.** Since the commanding general was **given to** driving a hard bargain, there was little successs in the negotiations that followed. His patience with the uprising had **given out** months earlier, and he did not want it to appear that he had **given ground** in his attitude toward the revolt.

6. Phrasal Verbs from **to keep**

> **keep one's word:** fulfill a promise
> **keep up** *(can be separated):* maintain
> **keep out:** avoid, stay away from
>
> **keep track of:** make a record of
> **keep time:** run accurately
> **keep house:** manage a house

During summer, Marther **kept her word** by **keeping up** John's house while he was in Spain. When he left, she told him to **keep out** of trouble in Europe and advised him to **keep track of** his expenses. She gave him a going-away present: a watch that she hoped would **keep time.** Then she settled down to **keep house** for two months.

7. Phrasal Verbs from **to set**

> **set aside** *(can be separated):* save, place to one side
> **set up** *(can be separated)* devise, conceive
>
> **set out to:** try to
> **set straight** *(can be separated):* correct or reform someone

The couple planned to **set aside** some money before getting married. They set up a plan so that they would **be all set** to marry in six months.

But they experienced a disappointment after an automobile accident. When Ruth wanted to go ahead with the ceremony, Roger **set out to** convince her to wait. His argument **set her straight.**

8. Phrasal Verbs from **to check**

check out *(can be separated)* leave some place
check into: register at some place

check with *(can be separated):*
check up on: investigate
check around: ask repeatedly

Because he was feeling tired all the time, Cary decided to have a physical exam. He **checked out** of his hotel and **checked into** a clinic. After **checking with** a doctor, Cary began to **check up on** whether or not the clinic was licensed. He **checked around** to get some information.

9. Phrasal Verbs from **to get**

get ahead: prosper, succeed
get out of: leave
get a move on: hurry

get behind: be slowed down in doing something
get hold of: exercise self-control
get going *(can be separated):* speed up an activity

Lucien thought the best way to **get ahead** was to **get out of** Chicago. When the hot summer arrived, he decided to **get a move on.** When he **got behind** in his packing, though, his father told him to **get hold of himself** and **get going.**

10. Phrasal Verbs from **to make**

make headway: progress in an activity
make a living: earn one's income
make a hit: become popular

make way for: prepare for
make up one's mind: decide
make room for: prepare oneself for

Until she **made real headway** as a recording artist, Sheila was having difficulties **making a living.** Once her new record **made a hit,** though, the critics said other singers should **make way for** a new star. Sheila **made up her mind** to **make room for** some important changes in her life.

11. Phrasal Verbs from **to see**

see fit: decide, choose
see red: become angry
see about: think about

see through *(can be separated):* complete an activity
see to: take care of
see off *(can be separated)* say good-bye

When John **saw fit** to leave home, his parents **saw red.** They said they might even **see about** disinheriting him. His father said John should **see his education through** and **see to** his family obligations. After John said he would think it over, his parents **saw him off** at the bus station.

12. Phrasal Verbs from **to take**

take for granted *(can be separated):* accept as rightfully due oneself
take up something *(can be separated):* begin something
take a break: stop work to rest

take care of: be responsible for
take charge of: assume control of
take it easy *(can be separated):* relax

The young Army recruit had **taken for granted** the freedom of being a college student. But when he **took up** military training, he found few opportunities to **take a break** from the day's routine. During his first month of basic training, he **took care of** the dining rooms. Then he was asked to **take charge of** clothing and supplies. Only on Sundays would he find time to **take it easy.**

13. Phrasal Verbs from **to go**

go places: become successful
go without saying: to be implied
go from bad to worse: run down, deteriorate

go through: experience something
go to pieces: become distraught or hysterical
go through with: carry out, complete

Evelyn thought that, when she graduated from college, she would be **going places.** But it **goes without saying** that a person's expectations are sometimes not realized. After graduation, Evelyn's finances **went from bad to worse.** She **went through** a period of depression, even **going to pieces** on one occasion. Thing improved when she **went through with** her plans to look for a job for which she was well qualified.

14. Phrasal Verbs from **to run**

run an errand: shop
run out of: have one's supply depleted
run across: meet unexpectedly

run wild: be without restraint
run low: have a short supply of
run up against: encounter, meet an opposing force

Ellen was asked to **run an errand** by her mother, who had **run out of** sugar and milk. On the way to the store, Ellen **ran across** a vendor selling bananas. This caused her to **run wild** and buy eight of them. As a result, she **ran low** on money. When she tried to persuade the storekeeper to let her buy food on credit, Ellen **ran up against** some resistance.

15. Phrasal Verbs from **to bring**

bring about: cause to happen
bring in *(can be separated):* produce, yield
bring on *(can be separated):* cause

bring out *(can be separated):* emphasize, inspire
bring to bear *(can be separated):* intensify, focus
bring up *(can be separated):* raise, nurture

Prosperity was **brought about** in the Midwest last year because the wheat fields **brought in** a record crop of grain. This was **brought on** by an effective program of insect control and new methods of irrigation. Agricultural officials **brought out** the importance of continuing high productivity, asking farmers to **bring to bear** their best efforts so that they could afford to **bring up** their families comfortably.

16. Phrasal Verbs from **to look**

look up to: admire, respect
look like: resemble
look forward to: anticipate with pleasure

look after: take care of
look into: investigate
look out for: be alert for
look over *(can be separated):* review

George **looked up to** his instructor, who **looked like** his brother. Every day George **looked forward to** coming to class because the teacher **looked after** his needs. He **looked into** George's problems in understanding mathematics and **looked out for** any mistakes he might make. The teacher always carefully **looked over** George's papers.

17. Phrasal Verbs from **to let**

let down *(can be separated):* disappoint, betray
let pass *(can be separated):* overlook or disregard something
let go *(can be separated):* release

let off *(can be separated):* set free
let up on: moderate or lessen an action
let alone *(can be separated):* not troubled or bothered

Barry felt **let down** when he was stopped by a highway patrolman for exceeding the speed limit. He was relieved, though, when the officer said he would **let it pass** this time and **let** Barry **go** with a warning. Pleased to be **let off,** Barry drove away, remembering to **let up on** his speed so that he would be **let alone** by the police.

18. Phrasal Verbs from **to put**

put off *(can be separated):* postpone, delay
be put out by: annoyed
put over on someone *(can be separated):* trick or deceive

put to use *(can be separated):* make use of, utilize
put on *(can be separated):* get dressed in
put across *(can be separated):* convey, deliver (an idea)

The father **put off** repairing the plumbing because he was **put out by** the increase in labor costs. He felt that the service trades were trying to **put something over on** homeowners. Deciding to **put to use** his connections, he **put on** his best suit and visited the Better Business Bureau, hoping to **put across** his point and receive some assistance.

19. Phrasal Verbs from **to call**

call out *(can be separated):* speak loudly
call it a day: quit for the day
call up *(can be separated):* telephone someone

call off *(can be separated):* cancel
call around: inquire by telephone
call on *(can be separated):* visit
call for: require, make necessary

Barbara **called out** to me across the office to say that she was about to **call it a day** because of eyestrain. Then she **called up** her sister to ask her to **call off** plans for dinner. Instead of dining at home, Barbara planned to **call around** to find a good eye doctor she could **call on.** This **called for** hard work.

20. Phrasal Verbs from **to break**

break down: fail to function

break off *(can be separated):* cancel

break in *(can be separated):* try out the first time, train someone

break out: escape from

break through: penetrate

break even: neither gain nor lose

When we drove to Las Vegas, our car **broke down** on the way, and we **broke off** our plans to visit Lake Mead. In Las Vegas we **broke in** our new walking shoes by **breaking out** of the tourist crush along the Strip to stroll in the desert. At night we **broke through** the crowds in the casinos to try our luck in gambling. We finally **broke even** at the roulette table.

Answers to the Exercises

CHAPTER 1: TRANSITIONS
(pp. 14–19)

Transitions Pre-Test (pp. 5–6)

1. First,
2. Yet
3. Second,
4. For example,
5. Third,
6. So
7. In contrast,
8. Fourth,
9. On the other hand, Moreover, for instance
10. So, Then yet
11. For these reasons, At last, now,

Activity 1

1. For example,
2. So
3. But
4. First,
5. A lady there
6. however
7. Then
8. As a result,
9. From my story,

Activity 2

European universities and United States universities are different in many ways. **First,** European students enroll in fewer courses each term than United States students do. **Second,** European students seldom live at a university. **Instead,** they live at home and travel to classes. **Third,** most European courses are given by professors who lecture to their classes. **In contrast,** United States professors often ask their students questions or allow their students to form discussion groups. **Fourth,** European professors ask students to write fewer papers than United States professors do. **Consequently,** European students' final examinations are usually oral, whereas United States students take written final examinations. **Finally,** a European university is mainly a place to study. **But** at most United States universities, social activities take up a large part of the students' time.

Activity 3

(Alternate responses are possible.)

Foreign cars are often more expensive to own in the United States than American-made cars. **For one thing,** foreign cars cost more to buy. **Of course,** there are reasons for this. The quality of workmanship that goes into making them is very high. **Then** high tariffs on many foreign models have raised prices. **Furthermore,** foreign cars often cost more to register. **In addition,** insurance rates can be higher. **Moreover,** parts and repair costs are much greater than they are for American cars. **However,** there are some financial advantages to owning a foreign car. **First,** many of them get better gas mileage, and they need new tires less often than American cars do. **Second,** their resale value is higher. The price of a year-old foreign car may be only $300 less than what it cost new. **But** the price for a year-old American car will be around $1,000 less.

Activity 4

(Alternate responses are possible.)

Jane and Karen have many things in common. **To begin with,** both girls have the same background. Jane was born and raised in the West, and so was Karen. **Next,** both girls are interested in the same kinds of subjects in school. Jane likes French, history, and English. **In the same way,** Karen likes Spanish, history, and English. **Furthermore,** both girls want to be teachers. Jane plans to become an elementary school teacher. **But** Karen wants to be a high school teacher. **As you can see,** the two girls are almost like twins.

Activity 5

(Alternate responses are possible.)

Luis and Mario are different in three ways. **First,** Luis studies a lot. He wants to get all A's. **Otherwise** he wouldn't be admitted to medical school when he graduates. **On the other hand,** Mario rarely studies. He just wants a B.A. **Second,** Luis never has time for sports. He doesn't have time to play. **However,** he sometimes watches a game. **In contrast,** Mario spends most of his time playing soccer or basketball. **Third,** Luis doesn't like parties. **After all,** they usually last until 2:00 A.M. **And** he needs lots of sleep. **But** Mario loves parties. He gets to bed very late. **For some reason,** he doesn't seem to need as much sleep as Luis does. **In spite of their differences,** Luis and Mario are good friends.

Transition Post-Test (p. 21.)

(Alternate responses are possible.)
  1. First,
  2. For example,
  3. But
  4. Second,
  5. Because of this,
  6. As a result,
  7. Third,

8. For instance,
9. Fourth,
10. this
11. This
12. For this reason,

CHAPTER 2: SUBORDINATION
(pp. 34–42)

Subordination Pre-Test (pp. 23–25)

(Possible student answers)

1. The man **who escaped from prison** is missing.
2. Nobody ever tells me **what is going on.**
3. Pay close attention **when you attend the briefing session.**
4. The lie **that he told** cost Raul his job.
5. Here is an example **that you can learn from.**
6. The woman **whom I introduced you to** writes mystery novels.
7. **When Alex proposed to Sarah,** she wept with joy.
8. The sports car driver **who won the race** is my friend.
9. This year he worked harder **than he had ever worked before.**
10. The science fiction movie **which we saw last week** was entertaining.
11. **When you arrive in Quito,** send me a postcard.
12. The newspaper **that is published in New York** is delivered every morning.
13. The art gallery **where we met** is closed on Mondays.
14. The space flight **that was planned for Vensus** has been successful.
15. I am always wondering **why the universe took the shape it did.**

Activity 6

(Possible student answers)

1. The most important building **in town** is the post office.
2. I go to the post office to pick up my mail **after work.**
3. At the post office, I buy stamps **to mail my letters and bills.**
4. **At least once a week,** I go to the post office.
5. The post office is a good place to go **when you need to mail a package.**
6. You can buy a money order **to send cash safely through the mail.**

7. **If I have any questions about postal matters,** the post office will help me.
8. People **who need to buy stamps** can visit the post office.
9. **When I first moved to Ohio,** I rented a post office box.
10. I could open my post office box **if I remembered the numbers of the combination lock.**
11. At the post office you can get **mail from General Delivery.**
12. **If you are a stamp collector,** the post office often sells special issues of stamps.
13. The bulletin board at the post office contains notices **about criminals who are at large.**
14. **If you have the right change,** you can buy stamps from a stamp machine in the lobby.
15. I think I visit the post office more often **than I should.**

Activity 7

(Possible student answers)

1. **I didn't go to the movie** because I was too busy.
2. **The woman** who opened the door **was very friendly.**
3. **Sylvia washed her hair** before she left for school.
4. **We saw two deer** walking up the hill.
5. **The woman** sitting at the counter **is my doctor.**
6. **I had a conversation** with the lifeguard at the swimming pool.
7. Reading quietly, **I lost track of time.**
8. **Don't read that magazine** unless you want to.
9. **They found the missing frying pan** in the backyard.
10. **I can't remember** who telephoned you.
11. **Please wait for me** until I return home.
12. **Bruce Jenner,** a famous athlete, **has become an actor.**
13. **The notice** on the bulletin board **announced a 7:00 p.m. meeting.**
14. **I talked with a buyer** who works for a department store.
15. **Elliot went** to the fish market **to shop for our evening meal.**

Activity 8

(Possible student answers)
1. The woman **who is sitting at the table** is blonde.
2. The man **by the window** is tall.
3. The house **that we live in** is comfortable.
4. The building **that you see on the right** is a skyscraper.
5. The airplane **that we flew in from Madrid** was a Boeing 727.
6. The chair **that is on sale** is an antique.

 7. The car **that I am waiting for** is the latest model.
 8. The college **I have applied to** is coeducational.
 9. The grass **on that golf course** is green.
10. The ocean **at Hawaii** is very warm.
11. The child **whom we just passed** is laughing.
12. I go backpacking **at least once a month.**
13. The clouds become dark **during winter storms.**
14. The kitten is playing **with a ball of yarn.**
15. The wind is blowing **very strongly tonight.**

Activity 9

(Possible student answers)

 1. **Before** I go shopping, I make out a shopping list.
 2. She looks **as if** someone has told her a secret.
 3. I will wait **until** you finish your sewing.
 4. **When** you go to the store, buy a quart of milk.
 5. I want to go **wherever** music is being played.
 6. Paul returned to the house **where** he had grown up.
 7. **Because** February is a short month, Pamela works fewer hours.
 8. I will exercise **as long as** I have the energy.
 9. They saved money **so that** they could travel to Brazil.
10. He stood up **so** he could see the soccer game better.
11. **Although** Thanksgiving falls on a Thursday, we have a four-day weekend.
12. My brother has gone to school for more years **than** I have.
13. The barber **who** cuts my hair is busy for an hour.
14. Did you like the movie **that** we saw last night?

Subordination Post-Test (pp. 45–47)

(Possible student answers)

 1. The door **that leads to the attic** is open.
 2. We are walking **where the road narrows down to a path.**
 3. The woman **who is standing by the window** is well-dressed.
 4. Sergio is driving **while I am sleeping.**
 5. The time has come **when she must study for finals.**
 6. The concert **that we are attending** starts at 8:30 p.m.
 7. The airplane **which you missed** is taking off.
 8. The dog **that ran into our yard** is a German shepherd.
 9. That car, **which you see on the street,** has a turbo engine.

10. This book is interesting **because it deals with North American Indian cultures.**
11. The actress **who played in Lysistrata** won an award.
12. The lamp **that we bought at the fair** is new.
13. The boat sails tomorrow **when the sun comes up.**
14. Those sunglasses **that have mirrored lenses** are his.
15. These packages **that have been stacked in the corner** are gifts.

CHAPTER 3: Parallelism
(pp. 61–73)

Parallelism Pre-Test (pp. 49–52)

1. who asked us for directions/who gave us a candy bar
2. to explore/to decide
3. federal income tax/state income tax/Social Security
4. through the front door/up the stairs
5. to build model airplanes/to collect stamps
6. how to write a check/how to deposit money
7. when we planned to leave/what stops we would like to make
8. to play chess/to play backgammon
9. bicycle lanes/bicycle racks
10. in the classified pages of a newspaper/in a used car lot/in a new car showroom
11. from home/from a telephone booth
12. proposed marriage/gave Colleen a ring
13. typing/taking shorthand
14. wants to study/cares about graduating
15. leaving the dining room/running up to her bedroom

Activity 10

(Possible student answers)

1. **Hang gliding** and **parachuting** are sports I would like to try.
2. I like to read **science fiction** and **mystery** books.
3. We lit candles **in the kitchen** and **in the dining room.**
4. **Sicily, Rhodes,** and **Mykonos** are islands.
5. **Jogging** for three miles and **bicycling** are good forms of exercise.
6. Jaime **scuba dives** and **snorkels** in Hawaii.

7. My brother is talented **musically** and **artistically.**
8. **Attending the Mardi Gras** and **eating in fine restaurants** are two reasons for visiting New Orleans.
9. They **shared** a picnic lunch and **played** volley ball in the park.
10. Her sister is **bright, pretty,** and **talented.**
11. **Walking** to school and **washing** the dishes are my biggest problems.
12. Sarah looked at a **studio apartment** and a **one-bedroom house.**
13. We want a car that has **disc brakes** and **rack-and-pinion steering.**
14. To write a novel and **to earn** my Master of Arts degree are my goals.
15. When you **find** a dress you like and **decide** to buy it, let me know.

Activity 11

1. repair the old house/**build** a new one
   We can either **repair** the old house or **build** a new one.
2. star football player/**good student**
   Kyle is both a **star football player** and a **good student.**
3. reads newspaper advertisements/**shops for clothing.**
   After Sue **reads newspaper advertisements,** she **shops for clothing.**
4. **bought a bus ticket**/boarded the bus
   She **bought a bus ticket** and **boarded the bus.**
5. **unfair player**/poor loser
   Tim is an **unfair player** and a **poor loser.**
6. **install stereo speakers**/water hanging plants
   My two jobs are to **install stereo speakers** and **water hanging plants.**
7. inquire about a loan/**fill out forms**
   After you **inquire about a loan,** you will **fill out forms.**
8. a raise in salary/**a move to another city**
   He asked for **a raise in salary** and **a move to another city.**
9. intelligent/**ambitious**
   Jason is an **intelligent** and **ambitious** young man.
10. ride a moped/**bicycle**
    You can **ride a moped** while I **bicycle** to the store.
11. successful teacher/**outstanding coach**
    Mr. Crenshaw is both a **successful teacher** and an **outstanding coach.**
12. employment agency/**cafeteria**
    After we left the **employment agency,** we dropped in at a **cafeteria.**
13. to a laundromat/**to a barber shop**
    Before I went **to a laundromat,** I went **to a barbershop.**
14. flagged down a taxicab/**asked what the fare would be**
    We **flagged down a taxicab** and **asked what the fare would be.**
15. **ordered a Eurailpass**/bought airline tickets
    First we **ordered a Eurailpass,** and then we **bought airline tickets.**

Activity 12

(Possible student answers)

1. For Christmas I want either **new shoes** or a **windbreaker.**
2. We will leave for the beach either **tomorrow** or **the next day.**
3. Neither **my father** nor **my mother** has visited the campus yet.
4. The lost notebook was neither **in my locker** nor **in the classroom.**
5. He asked not only **for a larger allowance** but also **for a new car.**
6. Not only **Fred** but also **Albert** hit a home run in the baseball game.
7. We wrote off for both **a catalogue** and **a sample** of the material.
8. Both **my doctor** and **my dentist** are skilled professionals.
9. Let me know whether **lunch** or **dinner** is a better time to get together.
10. Whether **Rome** or **Cairo** is a better place to visit is up to you.
11. Although **she has her doubts,** yet **she is willing to try.**
12. Though **he officially stops work** on Friday, yet **he may work** for another two weeks.
13. If **she will practice** the piano regularly, then **she will become** an accomplished player.
14. We ordered either **a bowl of soup** or **a salad.**
15. Jerry decided to hang not only **a poster** but also **a map** on the wall.

Activity 13

This calls for original student response.

Activity 14

This calls for original student response.

Parallelism Post-Test (pp. 75–77)

1. She was **eating her sandwich** and **drinking her milk** at the table when I arrived.
2. We came across a cave that looked **safe** and **comfortable.**
3. When father **came** home with his boss and **found** the house a mess, he was angry.
4. Gloria knew that **patience, calmness,** and **affection** would quiet the child down.
5. David killed the snake with a big branch that he **had cut** from a tree and **had whittled** to a sharp point.

6. After the automobile crash, Ann lay in the back seat, in a state of **pain** and **shock.**
7. They hiked **for two days** and **for two nights** until they reached the mountaintop.
8. Tim **had expected** a negative vote and **had planned** to work around it.
9. We seated ourselves in the airplane, not in the **first-class compartment** but in the **tourist section.**
10. The dean is a man of **intelligence, humor,** and **wisdom.**
11. They gave Andrea the award for the best essay, **honoring** her and **making** her feel good.
12. Claude was **nervous** and **annoyed** because he had lost his keys.
13. It took the Greek warrior hero Ulysses ten years of **wandering** and **suffering** to reach his home.
14. Soon Consuela **stopped** worrying and **developed** a brighter outlook on life.
15. Dorothy had to learn not only **how to find** a job but also **how to keep** a job.

Paragraph Writing Pre-Test   (pp. 80–81)

1. This calls for original student response.
2. This calls for original student response.

Topic Sentence Pre-Test (pp. 87–88)

1) Depending on where they live and the shops available to them, North Americans today have three different ways of buying what they need.
2) This calls for original student response.

CHAPTER 4: TOPIC SENTENCE
(pp. 93–120)

Activity 15

1. Eating lunch is one of my favorite pastimes.
2. Baby-sitting with my little brother is no fun.
3. Implied: Driving a bus is hard work.
4. Not only can lightning strike twice in the same place, it is likely to.

5. Yet, whether people today realize it or not, they are still as dependent on animals and plants for their existence as their ancestors were.
6. For here we have a remarkable example of a plant that needs more than one shock to cause the tightening of the leaves.
7. English is full of words that have gradually changed their meanings.
8. Implied: Science has made great progress in the twentieth century.
9. Human blood serves the body in three important ways.
10. The woman's fear of scorpions made me glad that Ramon, a man who knew how to give injections of serum, was with us.

Activity 16

1) A. 3
   B. 4
   C. 1
   D. 2
2) A. 4
   B. 1
   C. 3
   D. 2
3) A. 2
   B. 4
   C. 1
   D. 3
4) A. 2
   B. 3
   C. 4
   D. 1
5) A. 3
   B. 2
   C. 4
   D. 1
6) A. 4
   B. 1
   C. 5
   D. 3
   E. 2
7) A. 3
   B. 5
   C. 1
   D. 4
   E. 2

8) A. 5
    B. 2
    C. 4
    D. 1
    E. 3
9) A. 2
    B. 4
    C. 1
    D. 5
    E. 3
10) A. 3
    B. 5
    C. 2
    D. 1
    E. 4

Activity 17

Because lunch comes in the middle of the day, it gives me a welcome break from studying. At school, lunch means thirty minutes out of class and a chance to rest after the morning's work. While eating, I can plan what I'm going to do in the afternoon. And besides offering a pleasant break in the day, lunch is always a good meal. **In fact, eating lunch is one of my favorite pastimes.**

Activity 18

Driving a bus is hard work. A bus driver must answer questions while guiding a bus through heavy traffic. All day long the driver answers the same questions without becoming angry. Every few minutes a bus driver has to ask passengers to step to the rear of the bus. In spite of traffic snarls and thoughtless passengers who cause delays, a bus driver is expected to cover his or her route on schedule.

Activity 19

English is full of words that have gradually changed their meanings. One example is the word "graft." The verb *to graft* first meant merely to work. English people once used the word in such expressions as "Where are you grafting?," meaning "Where are you working?" From this perfectly respectable meaning, the word has gradually changed. Today *graft* refers to illegal gains won by dishonest politicians. **"Graft" is a striking example of how many words have taken on new meanings over the years.**

Activity 20

My parents have gone out for the evening. Just as I settle down to read or watch television, my little brother demands that I play with him. If I get a telephone call, he screams in the background or knocks something over. I always have to hang up to find out what's wrong with him. **Baby-sitting with my brother is no fun.** He refuses to let me eat a snack in peace. Usually he wants half of whatever I have to eat. Then, when he finally grows tired, it takes about an hour for him to fall asleep.

Activity 21

One important purpose of blood is to carry the substances that maintain and repair the body tissues. In this way, blood serves as a provider. A second use of blood is to act as a disposer, carrying wastes and gases away from the tissues of the body. Blood acts in a third way as a defender. The white corpuscles in the bloodstream constantly guard against and try to destroy bacteria and other agents that threaten the body's welfare.

Activity 22

This calls for original student response.

Activity 23

This calls for original student response.

Activity 24

This calls for original student response.

Activity 25

This calls for original student response.

Activity 26

This calls for original student response.

Activity 27

This calls for original student response.

Activity 28

This calls for original student response.

Topic Sentence Post-Test (p. 121)

1) Lumber is still an important business in the United States in spite of the growing popularity of synthetic building materials.
2) This calls for original student response.

CHAPTER 5: CONTROLLING IDEA
(pp. 128–136)

Controlling Idea Pre-Test (pp. 123–124)

1) 1. few qualities
    2. several different ways
    3. various kinds
    4. advantages and disadvantages
    5. many reasons
2) A.1.: three different ways
    Chapter 4:
    Chapter 5: } These call for original student response.
    Chapter 6:

Activity 29

1. different kinds
2. many ways
3. various reasons

 4. more festive
 5. plan
 6. different approaches
 7. to learn
 8. different ways
 9. methodical approach
10. Certain guidelines

Activity 30

 1. People keep pets for different reasons.
 2. All television horror movies have several things in common.
 3. The varied clothes that people wear tell something about their life styles.
 4. There are creative ways to take a bath.
 5. Comic books are written on many subjects.
 6. Blue jeans are popular throughout the world.
 7. Magazines are published on almost every conceivable topic.
 8. Several techniques help a person to become more poised.
 9. Successful surfing requires a certain kind of athletic ability.
 0. There are a number of ways for a person to develop a healthy self-image.

Activity 31

(Possible student answers)

 1. Step 1: **acting, cinematography, and screenplay**
    Step 2: The acting, cinematography, and screenplay of the film *Lawrence of Arabia* were of top quality.
 2. Step 1: the mountains and the desert
    Step 2: Our vacation trip took us to **the mountains and the desert.**
 3. Step 1: difficult situation
    Step 2: At the Rumanian border, Anne found herself in a **difficult situation.**
 4. Step 1: versatile musician
    Step 2: A versatile musician can play many **musical instruments.**
 5. Step 1: changeable moods
    Step 2: Whether or not I have a pleasant day depends on my **changeable moods.**

6. Step 1: unusual experience
   Step 2: I had an **unusual experience** yesterday.
7. Step 1: exciting game
   Step 2: My cousin taught me how to play an **exciting game** of cards.
8. Step 1: important decision
   Step 2: Keith made an **important decision** that will affect his career.
9. Step 1: three kinds of teachers.
   Step 2: My school experience has taught me that there are basically **three kinds of teachers.**
10. Step 1: track achievements
    Step 2: Bruce's **track achievements** at the Olympic Games won him worldwide recognition.

Activity 32

This calls for original student response.

Activity 33

This calls for original student response.

Activity 34

This calls for original student response.

Controlling Idea Post-Test (p. 137)

1) 1. a number of suggestions
   2. "old-fashioned" customs
   3. valuable services
   4. two strategies
   5. many benefits
2) A.1.: an important business
   Chapter 1:
   Chapter 2:
   Chapter 3: } These call for original student response.
   Chapter 4:

CHAPTER 6: UNITY
(pp. 143–166)

Unity Pre-Test (pp. 139–140)

One good way to relax is to practice yoga.

Activity 35

1. d
2. b
3. d
4. c
5. b
6. e
7. e
8. c
9. d
10. d

Activity 36

1. The dean checks into unauthorized absences.
2. Fourth, cotton is not as heavy as wool.
3. _____
4. Shopping bargains are easy to find in this free port.
5. Gold was first discovered in California in 1849.
6. _____
7. To visit some foreign countries, travelers have to apply for visas.
8. Phoenix gets much of its water from the Colorado River.
9. European countries seem to accept individuality much more than the United States does.
10. _____

Activity 37

This calls for original student response.

Activity 38

This calls for original student response.

Unity Post-Test (p. 169)

The New York theater is also in a decline.

CHAPTER 7: COHERENCE
(pp. 177–191)

Coherence Pre-Test (pp. 171–173)

1) 1. (−)
    2. (−)
    3. (+)
    4. (+)
    5. (−)
    6. (+)
    7. (−)
    8. (−)
    9. (+)
   10. (−)
2) (Possible student answers)
    1. There was rain and hail.
    2. She found a burglar in the living room.
    3. She is always looking at herself in the mirror.
    4. I was expecting a letter from my boyfriend.
    5. She was only going to eat one piece.
    6. He talked about his plan to reduce taxes.
    7. She didn't have to pay customs duty on any of the things she bought.
    8. He is studying Aleutian wildlife.
    9. She used them at the pond yesterday.
   10. They expected to find gold bullion.

Activity 39

1. d
   b
   e
   a
   c
2. e
   c
   a

         b
         d
         f
3. b
   e
   a
   d
   c
4. c
   a
   b
   d
5. d
   b
   c
   e
   a
6. d
   b
   c
   f
   a
   e
7. c
   g
   e
   h
   a
   j
   b
   f
   i
   d

Activity 40

1. Elizabeth's classmates knew that she would win the top award in chemistry during her senior year at Columbia University. First, she had studied chemistry during her sophomore and junior years. Second, she never missed a class. Third, she performed every required experiment in all her chemistry courses. Fourth, she always worked hard.

2. Coherent.
3. I had a terrible morning today. I slept so late that I did not have time to eat any breakfast. I tripped over a curb on my way to my political science class and tore my raincoat. In the middle of class, I discovered I had left my physics assignments in my locker. At the end of class, the professor would not let me go to lunch on time. I had not turned in my assignments, and he wanted to talk over this problem with me.
4. We must all use our right to vote. We should not be like the lady who knew all the candidates in a small-town election and thought they were all such nice people that she could not choose among them. When she went to the polls, she took her ballot and simply wrote on the bottom of it, "God bless you all!" Our candidates do not want our blessings. They want our votes.
5. On a map, bordered by other western states, Arizona appears to be only of average size. Yet Arizona could absorb all six New England states, add Holland, and still have more than enough room to tuck in Switzerland. Arizona is a large state. Arizonans have plenty of living room. But the state's population, although it is growing at a tremendous rate, is well below that of the city of Pittsburgh. It is only 638,000.
6. If you learn a new word every day, in a year's time you will have 365 new sources of power and pleasure. Why not start now? Look up the word *genial* in a dictionary before you leave school this afternoon. Use it correctly in conversation three times before tomorrow's class. The word will then be yours to keep. You'll be on your way toward making yourself a master of words. A good vocabulary, then, can give you a real sense of power and a feeling of pleasure.

Activity 41

This calls for original student response.

Activity 42

This calls for original student response.

Coherence Post-Test (pp. 193–194)

1. (9)
2. (7)
3. (3)

  4. (14)
  5. (5)
  6. (10)
  7. (8)
  8. (4)
  9. (1)
 10. (13)
 11. (12)
 12. (2)
 13. (6)
 14. (11)

Paragraph Writing Post-Test (pp. 195–197)

1. *Topic sentence:* Shopping habits in the United States have changed
   greatly in the last quarter of the twentieth century.

   Controlling idea: changed greatly

   Subordination:
   1. Early in the 1900s,
   2. But in the 1950s,
   3. Because the streets were crowded,
   4. when the first shopping center was built.
   5. built away from congested city centers
   6. Attracted by hundreds of free parking spaces,
   7. By the late 1970s,
   8. In addition to providing the convenience of
      one-stop shopping,
   9. Inside the Galleria,
   10. that rise for several stories above a floor-level
      indoor ice-skating rink.

   Parallelism:
   1. clothing/furniture/hardware/groceries
   2. drugstores/restaurants/shoe repair stores/and
      barber or hairdressing shops
   3. Too many automobiles/too few parking spaces
   4. Open space is what. . ./And open space is what
      . . .
   5. from downtown areas/to outlying malls
   6. benches/fountains/and outdoor entertainment

   Transitions:
   1. Early in the 1900s,
   2. This street
   3. Here

4. In addition,
5. These shops
6. But in the 1950s,
7. And
8. By the late 1970s,
9. In addition to
10. For example,

Unity and coherence:

The paragraph uses a time development to support the controlling idea of "changed greatly." For six sentences, you read about Main Street shopping in the early 1900s. Then the writer shifts to discussing mall shopping since the 1950s. A third shift in time — to the 1970s — introduces the concluding example of The Galleria. Because every sentence relates to the idea of changing shopping habits in the United States, the paragraph is unified.

The ten subordinated sentences, six parallel structures, and ten transitions contribute to overall paragraph coherence. Once the forward movement of the idea begins in the opening sentence, it never falters. A deft concluding sentence ties the paragraph into a coherent whole.

2. This calls for original student response.

INDEX